# Memory Lingers

# MEMORY LINGERS

Lynn DiGiacomo

WRITE LIFE PRESS
HAMPTON BAYS, L. I., N.Y.

The Write Life Press
Hampton Bays, L.I., N.Y.

Photography by Lynn DiGiacomo
Book Cover Design by Mary O'Brien and Lynn DiGiacomo
First Printing April 2025.

ISBN 979-8-218-64345-4

# Contents

# AGING ... SOMETIMES WITH GRACE

# Acknowledgements

I wish to thank Lise Barbeau Finan, my dearest friend, who always believed in me and encouraged me. Despite life's challenges, she has remained kind-hearted and upbeat—always with a smile on her face and a slightly mischievous sparkle in her eyes. She is the strongest woman I know.

I wish to thank Melodie Monahan, whose writing workshop I took at the Rochester Hills Library in Michigan, who gave me a safe place to write. The women I met there, who later formed the Wednesday Women Writing Group, started me on this journey.

The Southampton Writing Group, which started with a writing workshop at the Rogers Memorial Library facilitated by Carla Riccio, has been the wind beneath my wings for over fifteen years. I wish to thank Mary O'Brien, especially, whose expertise, hard work and can-do attitude helped make this book a reality and who has inspired me with her never-ending quest for learning something new, staying curious and enthusiastic. I'd also like to thank Paige Hurley at the Williamson County Library in Franklin TN for her invaluable assistance in the final formatting of the book.

I am forever indebted to my pal Joan Mazzu for her friendship and for the wise and witty insights and honesty that often put me on the right path in my life and in my writing—and whom I still miss greatly.

I'm thankful to have Debra Jensen in my life. The Tuesday and Thursday yoga classes have made such a difference to me for more than fifteen years. The friendships that have evolved from them have been an unexpected gift. To my fellow yogis—Susan Benson, Neva Setlow, Ann Ernst, Sigrid Meinel—Namaste.

My family: my two sons, Ernie and Randy; my daughters-in-law, Jeanmarie and Kim; and my seven grandchildren, Gina, Nicole, Paul, Nick, Alex, Sal and Olivia. You are a constant source of joy and pride. I hope that one day, when I'm no longer here and you are curious about the details of our lives and those who went before us, you'll be glad I wrote this book.

And finally, Ernie, my love, has supported me every step of the way—from the days I went back to college with two young sons at home, through the writing and publishing of this book, I have always been appreciative of how you've been there for me. You are my rock.

## Memory Lingers

Memory lingers
in the doorway.
She waits for us
to beckon her in
or slam the door.
  —*Lynn DiGiacomo*

# Introduction

What follows is twenty-five years of essays. In some instances, over the years, I have written multiple versions of a particular event or subject. Some of the following essays are combinations of a few versions, or some are about the same subject from a different point of view or at a different time. So please forgive me if there are a few redundancies.

As far as the genealogical information that is contained here, take note that it is as accurate as I could manage. Many of the names are spelled differently at various times and places. Dates as well. Information is as accurate as those giving it and those recording it and sometimes rerecording it—inaccurately at times. I found one child on a census recorded as being nine years old, when he was really nine months old when you looked at all the data. So take it for what it is and follow up if you are interested. Always consider the value of your sources.

Why Do I Write

Some ask,
"Why do you write
of the pain,
the loss, the sadness?"

To me,
it is so simple.
I want to find
the joy beneath.

# ANCESTORS

*Because they dared to leave family
and homeland behind, we are here in America.
If nothing else, there is strength and bravery in that choice.
Because they forged ahead and endured, we are who we are.*

# McPolin

My McPolin great-grandparents, Bernard and Anna, were married in Ireland in 1872. Bernard was born in County Down in 1851. Anna was born in Kilkenny in 1849. Shortly after they were married, they ventured across the ocean to the U.S. They came to Pennsylvania where Bernard worked in the coal mines in West Mahanoy. Their son Edward James (my grandfather) was born there in 1875, and their son Richard in 1876. In 1880, they are recorded as still living there. Bernard was injured in the mines, after which he moved his family to New York. In 1891, he owned a stationery store where his wife Anna worked as a clerk. Anna passed away in 1902, in Bronx, New York, at the age of 52. Bernard died six months later. I can only assume that he loved her dearly since he had inscribed on her tombstone:

ERECTED BY BERNARD J. MCPOLIN
IN MEMORY OF HIS BELOVED WIFE
ANNA MCPOLIN
BORN IN CO. KILKENNY IRELAND
APRIL 1, 1849, DIED FEB. 3, 1902.

They weren't wealthy, and such a tombstone probably was quite costly. They had been married 30 years. They are buried in Old St. Raymond's Cemetery. I have written a tale of how it might have been, based on these basic facts and some research I did on mining in Pennsylvania.

# Bernard

He had been shaped by mountains, sky and ocean—the wildness of Ireland. The ocean waves breaking sharply without care to what or where they broke, washing ancient rock out to sea. Relentless. This land birthed a breed unsuited to the close quarters of mines—the black tunnels and coal and breathless air.

He sucked in air to breathe. He walked pitching forward in a breathless motion, gulping in short pockets of air. He was a squat solid man, red haired, shocking to see in the colorless landscape of the Pennsylvania mines, and blue eyed like the Irish sky he had left behind, eyes not yet hollowed by the mines in which he worked.

In the crossing he had not known he was leaving sky behind —could not have imagined. Yet here in Pennsylvania, the piles of slag from the mines blocked the sun and brought night on early, so that he entered the mines in the dark and emerged from them in darkness.

On the boat from Ireland there had been those who looked back at the mountains and the coastline, wistful, and there had been those who looked out to sea in search of a new horizon. He had been one of those. He had looked at the vastness of the ocean and built dreams upon it.

# Anna

From Kilkenny in the southeast area of Ireland on the River Nore, you, Anna McPolin, came. Newlyweds almost, but fierce and determined, you left family and church behind. You huddled together with others in the bowels of a ship to escape hunger and poverty. What was it like to be bound together in such a way—you and your husband Bernard—among strangers who were retching from seasickness? No going back, headed instead for a dream—of freedom, of opportunity. Headed for America.

Liberated finally from the ship, you huddled first in a holding area at Ellis Island, then to an examination area for prodding and poking, then to a train car headed to Pennsylvania where your husband was promised a job.

You found yourself living in a shanty in West Mahanoy, a coal town in western Pennsylvania. Alone, you gave birth to your son Edward and silently cried for your mother. Hemmed in by mountains of coal waste, dark and barren, that rose on either side so high that the sun rarely shone. Everything finely coated in black soot, you waged an endless battle to keep it at bay. Yet it seeped into the linen, your clothes, even your sleeping baby—everything. Fifteen months after your first son was born, your son Richard was born.

When the boys were four and five, Bernard was hurt in the mine. You prayed. How would you live?

Neighbors helped, but you feared each day that they, struggling too, would no longer be able to do it. You feared, too, that you would be thrown out of your house if he couldn't go back to work soon. Only working miners were entitled to live there.

He finally did go back and the days melted into each other, like oozing tar you got stuck in if you tried to leave. Wages were low, company store prices high. A slow eroding of hope.

Days turned into years and you feared that your eldest son would soon work in the mines and would come home, face black, the light gone from his eyes.

You knew it was time to leave.

*Andy Newman, of the* New York Times, *in one of his
columns once observed that there is a sense of lonesomeness
at the last stop–a bar, sometimes a deli and often
a cemetery. It made me think of the last stop of the El train
where my father used to get off when he came home
from work, where there was, indeed, a bar, a grocery store
and, across the street, the Woodlawn Cemetery.*

# The End of the Line

For years my father worked for the New York City Railroad. In the evening he took the elevated train, the El, to the end of the line at Jerome Avenue, across the street from Woodlawn Cemetery, at the edge of the Bronx.

He crossed the street to take the bus to the end of the line at the border of the Bronx and Westchester. He walked up Kimball Avenue, lunchbox in hand, to No. 220.

Here on November 11, 1970, at the age of 59, it was his own personal end of the line. When I think of him sitting at the dinette table on Veteran's Day in 1970, it makes me sad to think of him there, dying alone, a beer in one hand and a cigarette in the other—even though both of these had hastened his death.

This line of the McPolin family in the U.S. started when Bernard Edward McPolin traveled from Ireland with his young bride, Anna, to the coal mines of West Mahanoy, Pennsylvania, seeking a better life.

His son Edward James was born in Pennsylvania on October 3, 1875. The 1880 Census found Bernard "temporarily disabled" from a mining accident.

At some point during the next ten years, Bernard moved his family to New York City, where he identified himself on the census as a stationer; he eventually opened his own stationery store—a slice of the American Dream.

Edward married Elizabeth A. Ryan on Dec. 31, 1902. She was

the daughter of Anna Power Ryan and Richard Ryan. The family story is that Richard was killed while working on the Poughkeepsie Railroad Bridge, which was constructed between 1886 and 1889. Elizabeth's sister Catherine married Edward's brother Richard. Sometime before 1920, Edward and Elizabeth were able to purchase, with mortgage, their own home at 509 West 165th Street—another slice of the American Dream. But later, after the Stock Market Crash, they were living in a small apartment above the Kent Candy Store on McLean Avenue.

My father, Bernard Edward, was born in 1911. He joined an older sister, Anna, and an older brother, James. Younger brothers, Francis and John, came along in 1915 and 1917.

My Uncle Jimmy married. They had one son, James Jr., who from the age of sixteen traveled around the world as a crew member on merchant ships. Eventually he settled down, got married and had two daughters. Having been an oiler on ships, he found work servicing elevators for Otis Elevators. He died in a tragic accident at the age of 30, falling down an elevator shaft—without a son to carry on the name.

My Uncles Johnny and Frankie never married. Both died in another tragic accident in 1956. They drowned in the muck of the Hudson River when they dove into mud at a shallow part of the river in an attempt to save their dog, whose leash had gotten caught on the pier. The dog survived; they didn't. No sons on those branches.

My father, then, was the last hope. When he came home alive, but broken, from the Pacific after WW II, he and my mother had a son in 1948. They named him Gary. My brother, my kind-hearted brother with the proverbial heart of gold, worked hard for many years for the State of New York until disabilities forced him to retire early. Two short marriages, always struggling with his demons and to find love, he died of cancer at the age of 56. No children.

End of the line.

# Family Tree

How does a tree stretch across oceans? The seed grown in Ireland, then stunted there by the famine that turned potatoes black and starved the souls as well as the bodies. Trails of death were left in its path. Bodies uncounted, unburied, abandoned without marking their existence. How did you, my ancestors, survive?

The instinct for survival must have been strong, for some did survive. Did those who lived suffer survivors' guilt? Did it take something from them? Some crossed the North Sea to Scotland, to replant in new soil, in an attempt to grow. Saplings going farther still, across the Atlantic, cutting roots to do so. Root and sapling separated forever. What effect did that separation have?

Transported to the hard pavement of New York City, others to the coal mines in Pennsylvania. Both light-starved—hardly an environment in which to flourish. Watered by beer and whiskey and lost hopes, it is amazing that they survived at all. But the tenacity and instinct for survival of those famine forebears ran through their roots as well, emerging tentatively at first, then gaining strength and taking root.

# Hannigan

## From Donegal

My Hannigan ancestors came from County Donegal, the town of Letterkenny, a town in the Republic of Ireland—my great-grandmother's family was from Glencar, my great-grandfather's from Killyclug.

Donegal is an area that was hit hard by the Great Famine. It's a place I was told, "where they eat dirt, stones and all." The Famine started in 1849 and its effects were still being felt a number of years later. The famine killed one million people.

My great-grandfather, Patrick, was born in 1860 in Killiclug, Donegal. His father was John Hannigan, born 1844, his mother was Anne Gallaugher, born 1846. On Nov. 14, 1879, Patrick married Mary Ann McDermott, born 1859 in Glencar Scotch. Her father was William McDermott, her mother Ellen Carbury.

Sometime around 1881, Patrick and Mary Ann and their young son John made the move to Dumbarton, Scotland, crossing the North Sea to find work. My grandmother, Rose Ann Hannigan, was born in Cherry Tree House in Dumbarton, Scotland, on Oct. 16, 1885.

When we visited Scotland, we went to the library to find out information about Cherry Tree House. We saw a picture of it, and though it no longer stands we were able to find where it had been because it was situated between the railroad overpass and St. Patrick's Church. It was exciting to find the exact location of my grandmother's birth.

# My Grandmother

Roots grow deep when the winds are strong. I think of Nonie, my grandmother, Rose Ann Hannigan, born in Dumbarton, Scotland. I think of her, firmly planted, solid, stoic. I think of the winds that had blown in her life to make her so.

I think of her existence in Scotland, in a tenement in Springburn, Glasgow. I try to picture what it was like, how it would compel three sisters and one brother to leave all they had known, to leave family and friends, knowing that in all likelihood they would never see them again.

I think of her, a young woman of twenty-four, arriving in New York in 1910 alone, turning her back, squaring her shoulders, all her belongings in her hand, putting one foot in front of the other, each step separating her from her mother and father, who may have stood watching her disappear in the distance, waiting for her to turn around and wave one last time. But I don't think she did.

I don't think she ever looked back. I picture her—back straight, firm set of jaw, valise in hand, a determined look on her face and not a tear in her eye.

Years later she would fill out a form and refer to her origin as American, while her younger sister still put British. My grandmother's roots ran deep, not in the land of her birth, but in the land where she was replanted.

When she arrived, she had twenty-five dollars in her pocket. I know that she belonged to a Catholic organization that helped other women come here, so she probably came with the help of that organization as well.

For an immigrant woman she was well-educated; she could read and write while many in her class could not. She was trained as a nurse at the Royal Infirmary in Glasgow, though she never worked as a nurse in the U.S. I have a picture of her in nurse's garb, dress to the floor and a long apron over it. At that time, the nursing profession was considered quite shocking, some considering it close to prostitution because the women could see and perhaps touch men's bodies.

Sometime around 1912 or 1913, she met and married William Beauregarde Groomes, a tall handsome man with a handlebar mustache. As a plain, hard-working woman in her late twenties (which, at the time, was considered late to marry), she must have thought she was lucky. But he turned out to be a difficult, fanatical man. He was a Jehovah Witness who tried to keep his children isolated from the surrounding community.

She worked most of her life as a cleaning woman, down on her knees scrubbing floors and up on a ladder cleaning windows. For years, she worked in the rectory cleaning for the priests. During the Depression the priests, I was told by my mother, had steak and eggs for breakfast, while at home my grandmother and her children went hungry.

She was tough when she needed to be, and she often needed to be. Like the time during the Depression, when she barely had enough food to feed her six children and the cat had kittens. She knew if they lived that the kids would sneak morsels of food to feed them. She knew what she had to do as she one-by-one wrung their necks. To her it wasn't a choice. My mother never forgot or forgave her for it.

When I was little, she helped raise me while my mother worked. She cooked and cleaned, then sometimes she and I would walk about a mile, take the trolley to Getty Square, where my Aunt Horty lived, and she would help her. She worked hard all her life. But once in a while, at a party, someone would play an Irish jig and she would get a glint in her eye and lift the edge of her skirt up and dance.

When I was in grade school, she fell off a ladder while cleaning a second-story window in a big house across the street from Van Cortlandt Park. She was told she would never walk again. But my grandmother proved the doctor wrong.

Always stoic and undemonstrative, I can't say I actually felt loved, was never hugged or kissed, but I knew she was always there for me. And some of the things she did, I realized, in retrospect, how much they meant. When I got married, she bought me a fancy dresser set—a mirrored tray with gold trim and two gold-trimmed perfume bottles—because she knew I loved and wanted it. It was really a terribly impractical gift, and she was not given to do impractical things.

I would stop by and visit her after I got married, and she would take a dollar or two out of her little purse—not really so much at the time, but a lot for her. She would press it in my hand and pooh pooh any thanks I tried to give her.

When I was first married and we were living with Ernie's parents, the first time it rained, she walked around the corner and down the hill in the rain and up two flights of stairs, rang the bell, handed my "galoshes" to Ernie's mother and said, "Marilynn might need these."

She turned around and walked back up the hill.

Now, that's love.

# Nonie

My grandmother, Nonie, the source. Stories not told.

Sssssh . . . she holds her finger to her lips, turns away from questions, doesn't want to go back—to the old country, to the rain, to the dampness, to the left-behind life. She forges on, stoic in her strength, embracing neither it, nor me. The pushing-away words: "Oh, go on now." Maybe afraid of what might happen if she lets the pain out, she keeps it in.

I asked her once if she had been happy. She looked up as if she didn't understand the question and said, "Oh, go on now" with her eyes. The question hung between us like words foreign to the tongue—incomprehensible. I, the asker, ashamed of the question, understanding in the silence the language without words that filled the room.

She always said she didn't want to go back to the old country. And yet, the one story she told again and again toward the end of her life is the one that returns her to the old country, to the bogs of Ireland, where she is lost and cannot find her way.

Then the fog parts and opens up a path leading her home.

# By the Seaside

On one of the last days of summer, I sit at the water's edge and let the lapping waves of the bay gently wash over me. I think of my grandmother and her "old ladies" bathing suit, doing the same in Seaside Heights, New Jersey, when I was a teenager.

She either sat there at the water's edge or on a bench on the boardwalk, saying that she was too old to join us in our beach activities.

As I sit here, I wonder if she got the same sense of joy and contentment in this simple pleasure of sea and sand and sky. Quiet pleasures I would never have guessed existed as a young teen.

I was all about the thrill of the electric-lit nights of the board-walk, the honky-tonk music, the bad-boy types spinning wheels of chance and seeming to offer more than the carnival prize—the promise of a kiss under the boardwalk perhaps, their eyes seemed to say.

Nonie, probably about my current age at the time, sat for hours on that bench, uncomplaining. No book. No cell phone. Did she people watch? Make plans (pick up a prescription, visit a friend, go to church) as I often do when sitting somewhere without any other distractions.

Somehow, I think not.

I think, after all the hard work she had done over a lifetime —raising six kids, cleaning houses for herself and others as a housekeeper, cooking and cleaning for my mother who worked, helping to raise me and my brother—that she deserved to do nothing at all.

# Groomes

William Beauregarde Groomes was born in New Haven, Connecticut on March 16, 1888. He was a letter carrier in NYC. His father was William B. Groomes, born c 1865, and his mother was Elizabeth Smythe, born c 1865 in Ireland (Free State).

After William's birth his father married Ida Tice. They had two children, Charles and Wilhelmina (two half siblings he never knew).

William's mother, Elizabeth, married Robert Moore, who was a businessman. William had a half-sister from this union: Mildred Moore Morrison.

In 1930 my mother's grandparents, Robert and Elizabeth Moore, owned a home valued at $19,000 and had a live-in maid. Yet when they visited he would bring her and her siblings pencils from his place of work. She told me they were hungry, and you couldn't eat pencils.

William's grandfather was George C. Groomes, born in Isle of Ely, Cambridge, England. He married Mary Plunkett in Hartford, Connecticut in 1851. His father was Joseph Groomes, born c 1797 in Cambridgeshire, England, who married Elizabeth Thimbleby in 1820.

My mother's father, William, always wondered about his family. His mother, however, never talked about his father, so he was unaware of his lineage or that his father and his new family lived nearby in New Haven.

# Peonies and Roses

I see your photo, Mother,
standing in the yard on Kimball Avenue,
arm raised on the limb of a tree,
in your crepe de chine dress,
glamorous against the backdrop
of the old, shingled house.
Waiting for Prince Charming.

You will meet him
riding in on his motorcycle,
not a trusty steed.
He is there to save you, you think,
but who will save him?

Sides will be taken.
Neither will win.
No hint of war, of drink,
of words that cut like knives,
only the sunshine on this beautiful day,
in a garden filled with peonies and roses.

# My Mother

My mother, Mildred Veronica Groomes, was born on Jan. 3, 1919, in Yonkers, New York. She was the second oldest child of William Beauregarde Groomes and Rose Hannigan. William was a tall stern man, a Jehovah Witness, who would be a very strict and controlling parent to his five daughters and one son.

My mother—intelligent, ambitious, and fun-loving—was eager to leave the restrictive environment of home. When she met my father—a handsome lifeguard with a motorcycle who was eight years older—he seemed like a prospect. They married in 1939 and had a few years of freedom, adventure and travel before I came along in June of 1943—a year and a half after the bombing of Pearl Harbor.

My father was thirty when the U.S. entered the war and had already served, but as the war lingered, he too got involved. There's a picture of him in his Navy uniform holding me as an infant. That's the last time I would see him till after the war.

He came home a different man, a different kind of husband, a different kind of father. His service in the Philippines had not only turned his hair gray, replaced his poor teeth with a set of false ones (because that was easier and quicker for the Navy than fixing them), but it had done something to his soul.

I sometimes wonder what it must have been like for my mother to see him for the first time when he came home from the war, a relative stranger who looked significantly older than the man who had left.

The first image I have of my mother is when she was sitting in front of her vanity, getting ready to go out for the evening. I picture her sitting, looking in the mirror, two glass boudoir lamps, one on either side, putting on her pencil-thin Greta Garbo eyebrows with her red Maybelline pencil. The dress she would shimmy into that night was her cocoa-brown crepe de chine cocktail dress, with slits in the sleeves, padded shoulders and fluid draped lines. She always seemed to be going somewhere—to work, to a meeting, for an evening out.

My mother taught me about fashion through her example and clothes she bought me. I have fond memories of my favorite outfits: a gray velvet holiday dress, a cute little set of jodhpur pants with a matching checkered jacket and a hat, a dress I called my ice cream dress because it was pastel-colored plaid, and many, many Easter outfits. I was always dressed to the nines.

When I was about six or seven, she decided to take the policeman's test in Yonkers, which was required to become a school crossing guard. She practiced and studied for that test with a vengeance. One thing she had to do was jump over a certain height. I remember her running across the back yard, with her long legs, and jumping over an ever-increasing height until she met the requirement.

She got the job and wore a blue uniform, with a white strap across her chest, a hat, a badge, and a real police whistle. Boy, was that whistle loud. A friend of mine told me that I used to say that my mother was so strong that she could stop a car with one hand.

Always good with figures, when my brother started school she began going to night school to learn accounting. At the time, she was working as a clerk at a business that burnt to the ground before she finished the course. She took advantage of the opportunity and applied for a job as an accountant. She soon found out, though, that she couldn't get a job as an accountant without experience.

With a little hutzpah and some luck, she told one employer that she had worked as an accountant at the place that had burned down. Because all their records were destroyed in the fire, they were unable to verify that. They hired her anyway. Each night for quite a while she came home and studied her accounting books to make sure she was doing it right.

She kept that job for a number of years, before working as an accountant and retiring from Pepsi Cola Headquarters in Rye.

Another gutsy thing I remember she did was to help my grandmother get her Social Security.

My grandmother worked most of her life as a cleaning lady at the rectory for the priests and in a few private homes, but she had no record of any of those jobs. She started working, cleaning a bank in Getty Square at night in order to qualify for Social Security.

She was a few months away from the required working time when she had a terrible fall from a ladder while cleaning second-story windows. My mother came up with the idea that she and three of her four sisters would alternate cleaning the bank for her for the few remaining months so that she could get Social Security. Since my grandmother had a key for the bank and there was no one else there at night, no one would be the wiser.

I went with my mother once or twice and remember the bank well. I was awed. There was a big clock and gold designs on the entrance. The main floor had marble floors and ceilings that seemed to reach to the sky. When I looked up at the ceiling, it was golden with designs and lights hanging down. The elevators that would take us downstairs were fancy gold ones. Downstairs there were a lot of little cubicles in a room with a gate. My mother said that's where rich people kept their important things. It was exciting and scary being at the bank at night with no one else there.

# DiGiacomo

When I married into the DiGiacomo family, I was interested in their journeys to the United States and asked my mother-in-law many questions. Family stories are important. Through them we learn where we've come from, and perhaps to understand family dynamics. My sons share the DiGiacomo genes, as well as my mother-in-law's Pinelli genes, so this is part of their legacy.

## From Salerno They Came

Alessandro (Alexander) DiGiacomo was born on April 1, 1883, in Salerno, Italy, the son of Aniello DiGiacomo and Giustina D'Amato. On November 19, 1903, he married Antoinetta Buongiorno, born in Italy Jan. 14, 1888, the daughter of Antonio Buongiorno, mother's maiden name Sabattello. They had four sons.

Two sons were born in Italy: Aniello (Neil), born in Salerno, Nov. 12, 1906; Emilio (Dick), born in Giovi, Salerno, in 1909. On Aniello's birth certificate, Alessandro is listed as a *pizzicagnolo*, a delicatessen owner.

Alessandro emigrated to the U.S. on May 3, 1910 during a wave of Italian immigration, age 27, wife stated as Antonia Buongiorno. Stated destination was to cousin Fidele, age 28.

His wife, Antoinette, arrived two-and-a-half years later, on Oct. 26, 1912, along with sons Aniello, age 6, and Emilio, age 3, residence Salerno, destination was to Fedele DiGiacomo at 907 10th Ave., New York.

Their son Ernesto Paul (Ernest) was born on July 27, 1913, in New York. Their youngest son, Alfredo (Alfred), was born on April 10, 1915, in New York.

In 1930, they lived in the Bronx, New York. He was working as a chef at the Fort Tryon Tavern at 5008 Broadway. Later he was the owner of a candy store and then a restaurant and bar.

While trying to break up a fight at the bar, he was hit in the head on Aug. 6, 1938, and subsequently died on December 19, 1938, at St. Joseph's Hospital (where he had been attended to since Sept. 23), in Inwood, New York. He was 55 years old. His son Ernest was 25 years old.

The bar was located under the EL in the Inwood section of the Bronx, at 3852 10th Ave. At the time, he lived at 714 Penfield St., Bronx, New York. He is buried in Woodlawn Cemetery.

Antoinette died from a fall in front of her house on 167 Glover Ave. on May 26, 1964, in Yonkers, New York. She was 76 years old.

# Coming to America

The city grounds down foreigners,
chiseling an American.

Hurrying through alien streets,
passing others without notice,
the old ways melt away.

Sunday's slice of time,
Is a hollow soon filled.

Alien words surround me.
Fireworks shatter the dark sky,
proclaiming liberty.

A life can paint a picture.
I pose before a gilt-edged mirror and
don't know the image.

Sighing indecision,
I question why I came

# Pinelli

## A Family Story

This is a family story that has kernels of truth wrapped in myth and passed down through the years. Stories handed down tell tales of hardship, luck, endurance.

The most fascinating ancestral story was of my mother-in-law's father and grandfather, Arturo Pinelli and Agostino Pinelli. It goes something like this: a man and his wife traveled from the mountains of Montelungo, Italy, to Buenos Aires, Argentina. In his village of Montelungo, high in the hills near Massa Carrara, Agostino was a stone mason. They were a family of stone masons. Pinellis had built the church in Montelungo and probably many others in the area.

Why did he go to South America to carve stone? Was he summoned? Was it to build a church? Or a monument? Did he go because the pay was good? Or for the adventure? Or because he would be blessed if he built a church? How many days by ship was it to Argentina? Was he aware of what the journey would involve or what the living conditions would be when they arrived?

While they were living in Argentina, they had four children, an infant who died, two boys and a girl. The story I was told was that the mother was nursing, perhaps lying on one of those dirt-floor settlements in Cordoba, where they were living. While nursing her baby girl, she was bitten by a snake and died.

The father sent the children back to Italy to be raised by his mother. I was told she was mean to them, locked up food from them, made them work hard. One day she was beating the little girl. Arturo, my mother-in-law's father, the oldest, tried to protect his little sister. The grandmother ran after him and in the process, she stepped on a rake that flew up and hit her.

The boy, fearing her wrath, ran away. He was only a young boy when he ran away—somewhere between eleven and thirteen. I wonder if he intended to run away for good or just till his grandmother's fury had passed.

He met up with an itinerant peddler and travelled with him for a time, then stayed with a family in Switzerland, who came to consider him part of their family. As he travelled from Italy to Switzerland, perhaps through the land Hannibal had viewed more than 2000 years ago, did he feel proud and invincible? Or, like the man with "no one" (as he would later put on the form at Ellis Island when asked for the name of a close relative), did he feel alone in the world?

After a time, he left to search for his father. This search would lead him to New York, to France, and back to New York again, where his father had remarried and settled with his new family. It is believed that his father finally settled in California, where he died and is buried.

This is the story, the myth, of Fernando Atilio Arturo Pinelli, born December 8, 1891—better known as Arturo or Arthur. I have seen a picture of a young Fernando Atilio Arturo; he looked very debonair. I have seen birth and death certificates and shipping and census records and have tried to piece the story together.

I am the granddaughter-in-law, wife of his grandson Ernest. I think his story should be told. It's an amazing one.

His parents were Agostino Pinelli and Clorinde Ambrosini, both born in Monte Lungo (long mountain); municipality of Pontremoli (ponte meaning bridge, tremolo meaning trembling, named for the shaky bridge over the Magra River); Province of Massa Carrara, renowned for its white marble used by Michaelangelo and for buildings in ancient Rome; region of Toscano (Tuscany) Italy.

Most in the family did not know that he was born Fernando Atilio; they knew him only as Arturo or Arthur. Even though Buenos Aires, where he was born, was and is in Argentina, records often show his birthplace as Buenos Aires, Chile, or simply Chile. In fact, my mother-in-law told me many times that her father was born in Chile. So, records as well as myths, as I've found, often contain inaccuracies, misspellings, incorrect ages and dates.

I knew Ernie's grandfather in his later years when he stood tall and proud and dignified. He was self-educated. He always worked hard to support his family, even during The Depression.

He worked as a chauffeur, and later as a furrier in New York City. He was a quiet man who had a loving wife and raised a happy family of two boys and two girls (Ivo, Isabel, Lydia and Robert). He had every reason to be proud.

Ernie and I visited Montelungo, on one of our trips to Italy. We drove high up into the hills to find this tiny village. Before we made the trip, Ernie's mom said, "Tell them you know Arturo Pinelli."

I probably rolled my eyes and thought, yeah, Mom, they'll remember a young boy who left there maybe eighty years ago.

When we got there, it was pretty deserted, but we did see a Trattoria Pinelli (closed) and a church (closed) with a plaque that said it was, indeed, built by a Pinelli.

Next to the church was a cemetery, so we thought we would investigate. No sooner had we started to search through the graves (which were quite interesting in that some had pictures of the people buried there on the gravestone), but an elderly woman came striding up to us and began to talk to us in Italian, in an obviously reproachful manner.

Remembering what my mother-in-law said, I quickly said, "Arturo Pinelli." Her whole demeanor changed.

"Arturo. Ah! The Long Island." And she started to rattle off some family names I recognized from my genealogical research, as well as other information in Italian. Unfortunately, neither Ernie nor I knew how to speak or understand Italian, so information about the family she had to offer would never be known.

She left us alone to walk among the gravesites and lament an opportunity lost

# Patterns

Family patterns. The pattern of our family of origin—the hooks and eyes of parents melding determines the pattern of the next generation. Straight pins hold us down to the pattern prescribed before our birth, to be cut from the mold. The thread of family binding us tighter, though the instructions may have been lost or obscured.

There are some, though, who reject the pattern, whose nature is slippery like taffeta or gossamer like gauze, who break the thread of tradition, open the seams and examine the structure, the pattern, who want to write new instructions, ignoring darts and markers. They don't want to be pinned down to a preordained shape of outdated molds and styles—or one that doesn't fit them—but instead to tie-dye a creative life without a pattern, just dipping in and experiencing and watching to see the awesome colors and designs that emerge.

Early on I decided to break the mold, the family pattern. I did not want the kind of life I had grown up with. Though there were some redeeming patterns in my family of origin, they did not outweigh the negative ones. I did not want my children to grow up in an environment of fighting and drinking and a loveless marriage. I did not want them to feel shame when they thought of family. I wanted them to feel loved and cared for.

I know I must have done something right, because my two sons are fine, successful men with outstanding families.

# CHILDHOOD

# June 25, 1943

I was born Marilynn Mildred McPolin on June 25, 1943. My mother was Mildred Veronica Groomes; my father was Bernard Edward McPolin. My middle name was Mildred, after my godmother, my mother's aunt and my grandfather's half-sister Mildred Moore Morrison. She lived in a big house on Lee Avenue in Yonkers and always seemed very classy to me. When she died, she put me in her will. She only left me $100, but I was so impressed to be included.

My mother had four sisters and one brother: Evelyn, Jean, Hortense, Rita and Robert. The family was very close when I was growing up—the aunts, uncles and some of my twelve cousins gathering during Christmas and on New Year's Eve; picnics at Blue Mountain, Kingsland Point and in our yard in the summer; outings to Rye Beach and on the Yonkers ferry; and always for my grandmother's birthday at our house, since she lived with us.

These gatherings did not always end pleasantly, mainly because there was usually a fair amount of drinking. They were, however, fun especially for us kids—with singing and my father playing the harmonica—and always interesting.

# I Was Born Innocent

I was born innocent,
plummeting into arms not ready.
The wall of granite
I was unable to climb.
Leaves fluttered with life
all around me.
I climbed trees for height and wisdom.
I walked through leaves with abandon.
I jumped puddles and walked through them,
testing, reaching, learning.
Half-formed and young,
I sought in the pages of books
and words of songs,
comfort and direction.
There were so many paths to follow,
so much to pick up from the pages—
words, lessons and cautions,
mine for the taking.
I kneel before the altar of words,
written for me:
I am worthy.
I am strong.
I am loved.

# Buried Treasure

I believed in buried treasure.
I dug holes in the sand and looked for China.
I sent letters in bottles
for foreign children to find.
I walked the pages of books
into ancient lands and exotic places.
I dreamed of princes rescuing lovely maidens.
I looked for magic everywhere
—except within myself.

# Childhood Was . . .

When my old bicycle was better
transportation than a limo.
When a bologna sandwich was a great lunch,
so great I had it every day of grammar school.
When going down the 'big woods'
was high adventure.
Or going to 'the Resey'
or down Coutant hill sleigh riding
was better than Vail or Aspen.

My secrets and worries were great,
but my ability to "whistle a happy tune"
was greater.

I was spy, sleuth, magic dragon,
king of the kingdom or damsel in distress,
when I opened a book and climbed inside.
Or when I went to the Kent Theater
and danced with Fred Astaire
or kissed James Dean.

My life then was an open book
waiting to be written.

# I Am From . . .

I am from nuns in black habits.
I am from alcohol and fights.
I am from "the old country"
of my grandmother
that I heard in her brogue and stories.
I am from longing and needing.
I am from books and poems and dreaming.
I am from strong women
and disappointments.
I am from puddles and dirt
and forts in the woods
and acorn fights and boys
I am from the deep sad lines
in my father's face
and his melancholy croon.
I am from the 50s and convention.
I am from the 60s and the music
and rebellion and hope,
and always the music.

# The Blizzard of '47

December 26, 1947—Twenty-seven inches of snow was dumped on New York.

I am 3 1/2. It is always noisy when my mother and her sisters get together. My whole family is at our house on Kimball Avenue for a holiday party. My grandmother, aunts, uncles and cousins are there too. I am excited and happy. My uncles peek out the window at the swirling snow and wonder if they will be able to get home.

Our house is a small one, but they were used to being cramped, since my grandmother had raised six children in this house when it had only two bedrooms and one bathroom. Soon everyone forgets about the snow and cold outside and gathers around the Christmas tree and in the kitchen. Trains chug around the tree.

In the kitchen, my father plays the harmonica. My mother and my aunts are laughing. My mother—tall, willowy, her dark hair swept up—is wearing a high-waisted black velvet skirt and a white gauzy blouse, tight around the collar, and pearl drop earrings. To me she looks like a movie star.

In the living room, there's a coffee table with a blue-mirrored top, and there's a fake fireplace at one end of the room. The wallpaper has maroon swirls against a white background. The room has maroon carpeting from the carpet factory where my mother works, a job she got when my father was away in the war and where she still works. The factory is a huge three-story brick building in downtown Yonkers, right next to the Otis Elevator factory.

My mother's four sisters are there—Evelyn, Jean, Horty, Rita

36

—and their husbands. My cousins too—my big cousin Ronnie who is 6; his little sister Pinky, a toddler; and Bobbi and Jeanne, both little babies. And my grandmother, of course.

The two babies spend the night in my room—one in a drawer of my dresser, one in my doll carriage—while the adults continue to party. My room is a small bedroom just off the living room. There is gray and dusty pink linoleum on the floor with hopscotch and nursery rhymes. On one wall is a child's roll-top desk, and there is a wood-framed blackboard with an alphabet across the top that you could scroll through if you turned the knob on the side.

Years later at a family wake, I would meet someone whose family owned the liquor store on Yonkers Avenue, about a mile and a half down the road. I was recalling the night of the blizzard. She overheard the story and said she remembered the storm too...and my family. She was a young kid at the time, and she had walked a mile and a half through the snow to deliver a bottle of whiskey to our house. Yes, that sounded like my family, I thought.

Under the frivolity and the celebration, there were undercurrents. Things, after the war, would never be quite the same. The women had gone to work—some returning to the home, others, including my mother, had not. They were different because of the experience. The men, too, were changed by what they had seen and done during the war, but no one talked about it. It was below the surface—another kind of storm.

# Walking in the Rain

When I was a little girl, I used to walk home alone from school—a trek of about a mile. I was an adventurous child who saw alleyways between buildings as hideouts for spies or havens for fairies. Puddles would invite me to jump over them or walk through them, regardless of the sogginess of my shoes afterwards. Chalked numbers on slate sidewalks were there to play hop-scotch. Piles of leaves were meant to swish through, perhaps once...or twice.

Dilly-dallying was my specialty.

My grandmother told me that if it ever rained, I should go to her friend Mrs. Foley's house, which was about one quarter of the way home. One day I traipsed home as usual, but that day it was pouring rain.

I was almost home when I remembered my grandmother's admonition and quickly turned around and headed straight back to Mrs. Foley's house.

Needless to say, my parents and grandmother got a kick out of my tale of returning to Mrs. Foley's. It was told over and over again as a funny story, though what was funny about it eluded me for several years.

# CATHOLICISM

# In the Name of the Father

In the name of my father and mother,
our first religion—our gods.
Transported here unknowing
to gods with clay feet,
I have to learn
to walk on my own.
In solitude to find strength
—unsteady god-child.
Trying to make sense
where there seems none.


Propelled, then, into a world of nuns,
In their engulfing black robes
and fearsome voices,
who take away the props
from this girl-child,
who sap the emerging strength
and intrude on the solitude,
imposing always their shoulds
and shouldn'ts,
with an authority
both longed for and dreaded.

They topple my simple
view of the world
with images
of bloodied hands and feet
and babies
with blackness on their souls.

# Kindergarten

I hold my mother's hand, but looming next to me is a voluminous black skirt. Beads dangle from its folds, and a cross. An arm swoops down and I see a stiff white tunnel. A hand emerges from the tunnel. It reaches out and tries to take me away from my mother.

I don't want to go.

Suddenly, she grabs me and I feel my mother's hand slip away. I search the faces, and can't find her anywhere. She is gone. I try to pull away. A tear falls, and I start to cry.

The black figure leans down. She is surrounded by a black cap, tied with a bow under her chin. I am afraid, but she smiles. "Come. You'll like it here."

I don't care. I continue to cry.

The building ahead is dwarfed by two taller buildings, one on either side. There's a garden we pass with a statue of the Blessed Mary. The passageway is long and wide. She opens the door and I am whisked inside.

Around me I see faces. Children's faces, but there is no one I know. They are playing and running around. Laughing. There are books, blocks and dolls and so many other toys.

Then, I hear her say dollhouse.

I hiccup. Dollhouse. I always wanted a dollhouse.

Then, I see it. The largest, most wonderful dollhouse I've ever seen. Three stories high. Taller than I am. And so many rooms. I head straight for it.

Suddenly, I forget about my mother, and missing her. It seems all right to be in this strange place.

# Passage

Sister Theodora and Sister Evangeline, twin pillars of the fifth grade. Large and looming, clad in the black robes of the Sisters of Charity, they monitored the second-floor hall of St. Barnabas Elementary School, looking for troublemakers. If you could get past them, like Scylla and Charybdis in the Odyssey, you could sail through the fifth grade to the eighth.

Many didn't. They joined the ranks of public-school students. A distinct memory I have of fifth grade is a lunch-time encounter with Timothy.

He spit at my best friend and me.

After lunch we went to Sister Evangeline to report his misconduct.

Feeling justified, we told her, "He spit at us."

After we explained what happened, Sister called Timothy over. White shirt, collar open, necktie askew, his face red and sweaty, he ran over when called.

A chubby boy with a big round face sprinkled with freckles, he cowed before Sister Evangeline's glare.

"Why did you spit at them?" she demanded.

Not having the foresight at ten to realize this question would be asked, I cringed as Timothy lamented, "They called me fat!"

"Well, you are, aren't you?"

We had an ally. I felt a moment of joy...until I saw the defeated look on Timothy's face.

Why do we remember certain tidbits, while others seem to pass unnoticed? Timothy, with his boyish chubbiness, lingers in my mind. Is it a reminder to speak thoughtfully? Is it about how much careless words can hurt?

Do we linger in his mind...the day two silly girls called him fat? Or the sting of Sister Evangeline's later insult? Or has he grown into that baby fat, risen to his adult height and self, and left us and Sister Evangeline long behind?

# Getting to Heaven

The indulgences cost twenty-five cents each. I wonder how many you need to get from Purgatory to Heaven. I think Uncle Bob might need more than one. I wonder how many I have to buy. Maybe I can ask Sister Gertrude when I get to class.

Rosalie bought one for her aunt who just died too.

Uncle Bob was nice and he was good to Nonie, so maybe he won't need too many. But I know he drank and said curse words. Are they venial or mortal sins?

When I get to class Sister is too busy, so I wait till Religion. I put my hand up and try to get her attention. She is starting to collect them—the money and the brown-and-white sheets of paper where you fill out the name of the person you think might be in Purgatory.

She is at Vincent's desk. He is handing her the money. She takes the money and the indulgence sheet off his desk, looks at it as she continues down the aisle, her brown beads clicking as she goes. "What is Pete's last name?" she asks loudly.

"He doesn't have a last name," he says timidly.

Sister whirls around, her black habit swirling, her rosary beads hitting the desk. She glares at Vincent as she lowers her head and strides towards him. "What do you mean he doesn't have a last name? Everybody has a last name!"

"He was my parakeet. He just died."

Before I can begin to laugh, Sister grabs Vincent's hair and drags him to the front of the class.

"You...can't...buy...an...in...dul...gence...for...a...bird...you   silly boy."

I don't think I will ask her about the indulgence for Uncle Bob. I'll just pray for him a lot to try to get him out of Purgatory.

# School

When the handbell rang, we lined up two by two according to height, class and gender, from one end of the street to the next in the morning and at lunchtime. We were to stand still and be quiet, both of which had always been difficult for me. Then we would march into school, one class at a time.

One day in particular stands out. I was always in the third twosome from the back. Behind us were the big girls—the girls I would today call tall and stately. Girls who sometimes stood with a slight crouch, shoulders stooped, thinking, perhaps, that three-quarters of the boys in the sixth, seventh and eighth grade were shorter than they were.

That day, my friend and I were disobeying the rules and talking to each other when a bee flew in my mouth and I cried out in pain and surprise.

Sister was there immediately and pulled me out of line in front of all the other kids and dragged me up the steep stairs to the principal's office.

I sat there crying until I was called into the office.

"What happened?" Sister Acquinata asked.

"A bee flew in my mouth and stung me, and it hurts," I said through my tears.

"What were you doing with your mouth open on line?"

"Um . . . I don't know."

"Well, go back to your classroom and think about it. And from now on, keep your mouth closed."

"Yes, Sister Acquinata."

LUNCHTIME

In grammar school, we walked down to the lower-level cafeteria, down stairs austere and cold—green-walled and worn-metal railed—jostling for place on lines, trays in hands, passing up the soup, which at the end of each day what was left over would be added to the next day's soup and by the end of the week would look unrecognizable. Some of us were lucky enough to have a mother who made us lunch. Mine were always the same—bologna sandwiches with mayo on white bread, wrapped in waxed paper and in a brown paper bag that somehow always got crushed amidst the books in my bookbag.

After lunch, we would emerge from our morning confinement—50-pound bodies of energy waiting to burst forth. Like people escaping from a burning building, we were propelled out of every door of the school. We were not to run, not to push, not to cross beyond the closed-off street in front of the school and the small park next to the convent—though they did close their eyes when we went into the woods across the street from the school. Here the boys tended to run in packs at lunchtime, calling themselves the red army or the blue army. The girls, wanting to be like them, formed groups too—calling themselves the red and purple gangs, and we vied for admission to those groups.

The real meaning of gangs alluded us, to us they were a way of bonding, feeling a part of a group, fortifying and energizing ourselves for the long afternoons of withstanding the challenges of the nuns.


TEACHERS

There were a few lay teachers. In whispers, some of us speculated as to whether our science teacher's hair was a wig, since it always looked exactly the same, without a hair out of place—parted in the middle, rolled up on either side, with the front in two odd-shaped curls sticking up on the ends.

We never did resolve the mystery if it was a wig or not.

The nuns were mysterious, too, underneath the folds of black they wore even in summer. We sometimes speculated if they had hair underneath their caps or were bald, what kind of families they had, what they were like before they were nuns. Mostly, though, we couldn't imagine them being regular people. Most of them never referred to a life before becoming a nun, so it was hard to imagine that they had one. They wore tight, confining white collars that seemed to constrain them. Some hid things, like rulers, amid their folds—or sometimes a hand that was swift.

There were those who felt some of the nun's ire most often. There was one boy in particular who had difficulty with some of the work, and he had his head knocked against the blackboard—probably only once or twice, but I sat there wordlessly watching, with the fear that it could or would happen to me. That image was etched in my mind so that it seemed to have been a daily occurrence.

More often, it was the wooden ruler that was the usual punishment. Here too, I'm not sure I was ever its recipient, but I could feel it on my knuckles just the same.

## PENMANSHIP

Doing things the right way...following the dots on the page, making the loops the same way they made their loops. Never could get it quite right...or didn't want to. Always was a bit out of step. Wanted to slant left when they said to slant right. Wanted to make my own mark on the page...on my life. Didn't want to be confined by the dashes and dots on the page. But I wanted to be a good girl, so I did. Until high school...when I decided it was time to be me and slant left instead of right. My handwriting was so distinctive that on a list of things each senior would be remembered for, one of the things mentioned about me was my "unique backhand scrawl."

# GROWING UP

# Days of Summer

We were eleven to fourteen during the summers of '54 to '57, innocents in an innocent time. Before the wider world beckoned us, the Hillview Reservoir on Kimball Avenue—the Resey to us—became our home away from home. The actual reservoir sat at the top of the hill, but our sanctuary was under a big old tree at the concave of the hill, just below a stand of pine trees and above the entry road. We would often sit under the tree on those languid, lazy days of summer—days of I-don't-knows, whaddaya-wannados.

It was August. It was August forever that summer of 1957. Waiting in the hot summer heat. Waiting while we climbed trees in the big woods. Waiting while we tumbled down the huge hill of dirt at the Raceway. Waiting for high school. Waiting to grow up.

In the hot summer afternoons, the pine trees were a cool Christmasey promise. By 1957, they became a refuge for our early boy-girl fumblings. The earth floor was cool under the trees, carpeted in pine needles. The rich scent of them filled our summer days, while hinting of its end. Boys of summer pulled us up the hill to tumble among the pine needles. We would play tag as an excuse for closeness that was still awkward. A rough hand would push up a skirt "by mistake" or touch a barely formed breast. At home at night, pine needles were wedged in my underpants, earthy with promise.

Just before summer's end, as the days grew chilly, one of the cute boys loaned me his jacket. It was black leather with all those little zippers, like the one Marlon Brando wore in *The Wild One*.

Ernie took it off, his thick wavy black hair falling onto his forehead. I put it on and it warmed me inside and out.

By the fall of 1957, members of our tight-knit neighborhood group, who had known each other since childhood, dispersed. Some of the kids went to St. Barnabas High School, others to Commerce, Lincoln, Saunders or Mount St. Michael. New friends were made, new groups formed. The big old oak tree was abandoned, waiting to be discovered by other boys and girls of summer.

# The Sugar Bowl

My grandmother had tea every day. She steeped it, added milk, then sugar from a round chrome sugar bowl. That sugar bowl sat on the Formica-topped dinette table in our house on Kimball Avenue for as long as I can remember. My grandmother had brought it home from her one and only trip back to Scotland when I was five.

My grandmother was a woman of few words, but we sat together after school and watched TV while the tea steeped. Often, we watched "The Guiding Light," "Arthur Godfrey," "Kate Smith," and, occasionally, "American Bandstand."

My favorites were the reruns of "The Loretta Young Show." She opened a set of doors and swished onto the screen in a different exotic outfit and glittering earrings each day. I held my breath to see what she wore, as she flashed her spectacular smile right at me.

On one very memorable day in 1953, when I was nine years old, we watched the Coronation of Queen Elizabeth II.

I recently looked up the definition of "steep." It means to soak in water thoroughly, also to imbue or saturate with feelings or opinions. You have to be patient to steep tea; I wasn't. But sitting there with my grandmother, watching her steep her tea and watching TV together, perhaps I learned some patience—and more.

My grandmother lived with us, and most of our family gatherings were held at our house. We celebrated birthdays,

Christmas and the New Year's holidays in that cramped dinette area.

One New Year's Eve, hats on heads, noisemakers in hand, we stood for a moment—three generations—and posed for a picture.

That chrome sugar bowl was a mute witness to it all.

# Two Brothers

I pause at the door, listening.

Silence. Good.

I heave myself in, drop my bookbag, the screen door slapping behind me, wood against wood, breaking the silence.

I know something is wrong the minute I see my father sitting at the dinette table, his head bent. He looks like he is crying.

My mother, standing next to him, looks pale.

My grandmother, gripping a handkerchief in her hand, looks up as I walk in.

"What's wrong?"

"It's Uncle Frankie...and Uncle Johnny. They're dead."

"Dead?"

The word rolls around in my 12-year-old mind as I try to grasp it. Dead. I know what it means, but it doesn't make any sense. I can't understand how not one person I actually know, but two, are dead...not sick and then dead, but just dead...all of a sudden.

"What happened?"

"They drowned."

Again, I am confused. How could they drown? They were such good swimmers.

So how could they drown? I feel something shift inside.

Instantly I know. I know the truth. They were drunk. As usual.

The next day I see an article in *The Herald Statesman*, "Two Die to Save Dog," with an old picture of my two uncles holding their dog.

2 Brothers Die
By Harry Altshuler,
Two middle-aged bachelor brothers—both
notable swimmers—drowned in the Hudson
River at Yonkers early yesterday in an effort to
save their dog which had fallen off the pier the
police believe.

Ironically the dog found safety. Although
the brothers are missing, the dog was found
whining by police on a crossbeam under the
pier.

John McPolin, 40, and his brother Francis,
43, lived at 33 Jackson St., Yonkers. Both were
plumbers. Another brother, James, of 10 Bell
Pl., Yonkers, said they were such good
swimmers in their younger days that both
often swam across the Hudson and back....

The next day at the wake, and the day after at the funeral, I hear
the same things over and over: such heroes, such a tragedy. I nod
"Yes...yes." It washes over me each time, waves of it...shame,
dishonesty, collusion in a nasty family secret. I am terrified that
someone will find out they were drunk...and that my father and
the rest of my family are drinkers too.

I wonder which one jumped in first...if it had happened fast or
slow...if they had had time to say an Act of Contrition.

In my young mind I am beginning to understand that the world
is not always what it seems, that things you read about in the
newspaper are not always the way they say they are.

Like a turtle, I retreat deeper into myself. I curl into books.

This "tragedy" haunted me for years, perhaps because there had
been no one I could talk to about it.

Later, as an adult, I realized that though it was a big story in the
papers for one or two days, few people outside the family realized
that they had been drunk.

And, probably, if I had asked anyone a year later, they would hardly remember the incident, and yet the shame I felt left an indelible mark on my character.

Shame is a more complex feeling than embarrassment. It is "the painful feeling arising from the consciousness of something dishonorable, improper, ridiculous." Embarrassment is a moment; shame can be a lifetime. It burrows under the skin and clings to the soul. The alcoholism in my family not only caused me embarrassment, but shame. It wasn't until the book *Angela's Ashes* by Frank McCourt, where alcoholism was spoken about openly by a respected teacher and scholar, that I realized that the shame wasn't mine to carry.

# Clang, Clang, Clang

I don't remember the day I got it, but oh, I remember riding it.

When I first rode it, I couldn't reach the seat, but I rode it anyway. My bike was also unique in that, even without a horn, it announced my arrival. Clang, clang, clang, it echoed, as the pedal hit the chain guard each time I pumped it. I pumped harder and harder—to go faster and faster. Taking me away, and taking me to new adventures.

I don't remember any of the other girls in the neighborhood owning a bike. Certainly my best friend didn't. Her father, from the old country, would never allow it. I think Mary Sullivan had a bike, but she was a few years older than I was. Most of the other girls were more interested in girlie things. I used to like playing with my dolls, but at eleven or twelve, I was more interested in going down to the big woods and seeing what the boys were up to. I had a sense of adventure.

Two of the boys in the neighborhood had bikes. Henry had a black and white Schwinn that he paid for with his newspaper delivery money. Ernie had a sparkling new green and cream Columbia bike he had gotten for Christmas.

Both of them took me for rides, sitting on the crossbar of the bike, tucked in between them and the handlebars. I loved the feel of the wind and the speed, and wanted my own.

My mother brought home a dark red used bike from somewhere, I'm not sure where. One day I came home and it was leaning against the side of the house.

It was a bit rusty and the pedals were worn, but it looked

beautiful to me. I bet I was happier with that old bike than both those boys and their brand-new ones.

I rode everywhere, fast, free and fearless. Though sometimes that got me in trouble. Like the time I wanted to get a running start on the hill on Kimball Avenue, so I thought what a great idea it would be if I started on the level side street, built up speed, then turned left onto Kimball. What I hadn't counted on was a car coming down the hill at the exact same moment I came speeding out. Suddenly I heard the screeching brakes, and saw the car two inches in front of me.

The driver jumped out of the car asking, "Are you okay? Are you okay?" It was the biggest scare of my life—his, too, I think.

I guess someone could have fixed my bike so it wouldn't make noise, but my father wasn't too handy and not too interested. But I kind of liked it like that. It was music to my ears.

Clang, clang, clang.

# Scenes from the Mall

Yesterday my daughter-in-law told me they had demolished most of the old Nanuet Mall in Rockland County, New York, to transform it into The Shops at Nanuet, advertised as a "vibrant open-air town center," a new kind of shopping experience with green space and plantings amid the stores.

My thoughts immediately kaleidoscoped back to Yonkers and the Cross County Shopping Center. I smiled and thought the old is new again. It, too, was an open-air shopping district that opened in 1954 when I was eleven years old.

My girlfriends and I had read in *The Herald Statesman* that it was the world's largest and greatest shopping center. It was only three miles from our neighborhood. My friends and I couldn't wait to go. For the next twelve years, many of my memories revolved around the Cross County Center.

During most of my teen years I spent many a weekend there. The Cross County Center replaced McLean Avenue, our local main street, as the neighborhood shopping area. Unlike McLean Avenue, where stores were built and opened at various times during the past century and where you parked on the street and usually went to one or two stores nearby, this strangely modern world was a planned shopping district, where you would park your car in the parking lot and walk from store to store at your leisure.

It was a precursor to the enclosed malls of today, one of the first of its kind in the United States. This open-air version had a wide, elongated town square between a row of stores on either side. The plaza was filled with shrubs and plantings, benches, and criss-crossing pathways. The first enclosed mall opened two years later in Minnesota.

I don't remember the first time I went to the mall, but I remember with remarkable clarity the day I thought I would be arrested for shoplifting.

The day started like any other. I hopped the bus with friends Jane and Joyce. I was fifteen; Jane was fourteen; Joyce, though the youngest at thirteen, was perhaps the boldest. She had shocked me one day when she undressed in front of me in her bedroom. This was scandalous to a Catholic school girl like myself, who was adept at getting in and out of my gym clothes without showing an inch more skin than I had to. I was agog at the sight of her young body and its budding little breasts.

Jane's parents were divorced, quite unusual back then. She lived with her mother in a tiny apartment on the top floor of a house down the block. She told many tales of how she manipulated her parents to get exactly what she wanted.

The three of us went to John Wanamaker's Department Store, whose wide entryway was flanked by two lions that towered over our heads, giving it a feeling of elegance and hinted at things we couldn't afford. I momentarily lost track of Jane and Joyce as I gazed at the sparkling jewelry in the display cases. My heart raced when I caught sight of them; they were slipping things into their purses, quickly and deftly. I didn't know what to do. I just wanted to get out of there, but before I could move, they were next to me.

"Go on. Take something. It's fun. Don't you want anything?"

Of course, I did, but I didn't want to steal. I just shrugged.

They continued their petty thievery. I finally broke down and grabbed a seventy-nine-cent Elvis Presley scarf. While they were skilled and swift, I was inept. Instead of slipping the scarf inconspicuously into an awaiting purse, I grabbed it then didn't know what to do with it. I opened my purse awkwardly and put it inside.

I got the three of us caught. The store detective came up behind me and marched the three of us up the escalator to the offices on the second floor, bringing our mini crime spree to an end.

I sat across the table from the store detective. I didn't know where to look or what to say. Big fat tears slid down my cheeks as they called my mother.

Jane and Joyce sat there scowling, sometimes at me.

It seemed like hours before my mother arrived, as we sat in silence, trying to avoid the hostile looks from those in the office. Finally, she strode in. Without preamble she glared at me and asked, "Why?"

Because I was the oldest, the detective told my mother I was the ringleader and should have known better. I did know better. I certainly wasn't the ringleader, though, but I remained quiet.

"Her father's out of work," my mother offered as way of explaining. Both of us knew that his being out of work wasn't the reason. There was no hardship with my mother working, just some belt-tightening.

My mother was an imposing woman—big-boned and tall—and after some discussion they agreed not to press charges but banned the three of us from the store for a year.

My mother and I drove home in silence.

I took the banishment seriously and didn't go near the store for the entire year. Not so my fearless former friends. I heard from others that they totally ignored their expulsion. I have a feeling they continued to shoplift, but it was the first and last time I ever did.

After my year of banishment, I discovered that Wanamaker's had glassed-in booths on the second floor where you could take 45rpm records you were thinking of purchasing and listen to them. It became a gathering place for me and my friends. We sang the words to song after song. We shook our ponytails and wiggled and giggled as we sang the words.

I guess the store realized that we teens were doing more listening than buying because the booths weren't there for long.

In F.W. Woolworth's luncheonette, I sat at the counter, lined with red vinyl-covered stainless-steel stools, and ordered an egg salad sandwich. I felt like a grown-up, even though I was tempted to twirl around on the stool.

I wish I didn't remember the Thom McAn's shoe store where I asked to try on a size nine shoe, and the cute young clerk chuckled and said, "Why don't you just go to Herman's Sporting Goods and get canoes?" I felt my face flush, but before I could think of a response, he had scurried off to get my size nine.

At Blackton's Lingerie Shoppe, I would ogle the fancy lingerie in the window. One day when I snuck inside and touched the delicate items, scenes of Rhonda Fleming in her lacy bras and Marilyn Monroe in her silky slip in *Some Like It Hot* and Sophia Loren in *The Millionairess* flitted through my mind.

I thought of the day I would be able to spend a whole dollar for a pair of lacy underpants, instead of the panties with the days of the week written on them that I wore.

The very first grown-up dress I bought with my own money, I purchased at Franklin Simon's with money I earned by baby-sitting three little ones for twenty-five cents an hour. It was kelly-green with a royal-blue scarf at the neck. I was attracted by the unusual combination of green and blue, which made it both elegant and daring. It cost $9.99; I had never bought anything that expensive before. I can still remember the softness of the jersey wool skirt.

In 1962, I got married to my high school sweetheart, Ernie, and for a time we lived with my in-laws. When we got our first apartment at 138 Alexander Avenue, we bought some of our furniture at the Cross County Center. There was a small specialty shop featuring the latest designs. Our apartment had a main room that served as a dining area and living room, as well as our son's bedroom, so it didn't have room for a couch. We purchased two Danish modern chairs—one bright orange, the other a blue and green flowered pattern—both of which had been on clearance. We also bought a room divider with shelves and a sleek black lion to sit on one of the shelves. We felt very modern and a bit avant garde since this was the latest style.

My mother-in-law worked in Wanamaker's at the time, so we got a small dining set and a tall orange table lamp at a discount to complete the setting.

A few years later, after I had our second child, I walked the three miles to the mall with my two sons, one walking and one in a stroller. I recall the walk home; I was tired but renewed by my old stomping ground. My older son, though, was just plain tired and had to hitch a ride with his baby brother in the stroller.

Around the holidays the mall became the backdrop for holiday photos as well as excursions for our young family. The Easter Bunny was there in the spring, along with the season's budding trees and flowers, and Ernie and I and the two kids posed in our "Easter outfits."

At Christmastime, the center aisle was aglow with myriad lights—at least fifty feet of green and blue and red and white spread out before us, beckoning. The kids were mesmerized by this sparkling wonderland.

"Mommy, Mommy, look it's Santa," they would shout when they saw him walking around in his red suit.

In 1966, we moved across the Hudson River to the no man's land of Rockland County—and three long years without a shopping mall. Suburbia in the 60s: no walkable downtown, no second car, little discretionary money and nowhere to go with kids in tow, especially in winter.

Then the Nanuet Mall opened in 1969. As I waited for the Grand Opening, my anticipation mounted. We had finally gotten a second car so on that morning I drove with my two sons, then seven and three and a half, who were uninterested in the shopping, but caught up in my excitement.

We got there early and waited with the crowds outside of the new Bamberger's Department Store. The prospect of being one of the first customers to shop in the new store and of my sons getting their little handprints in the concrete sidewalk next to the entryway was enticing. It was such a momentous occasion in my sadly barren suburban existence that I actually remember what I was wearing that day: a purple jersey mini-dress rimmed with red. Perhaps it is cemented in my memory by a comment I overheard that a little girl made to her mother.

"Mommy, that lady is wearing purple and red. Those colors don't go together!"

I looked at her and smiled and secretly took pride in my love of and ability to put together unusual color schemes.

As I sat with my daughter-in-law, I thought of those tiny handprints in the concrete by the entryway and wondered if they were still there after the mall was demolished. After all, Bamberger's, now Macy's, was still there.

I mentioned it to my daughter-in-law, and she said that she and her mother had been at the opening of the Nanuet Mall too. I laughed and said maybe she and my son had been eyeing each other back then.

After my son and daughter-in-law left, I thought of that little outspoken girl who had commented on my dress and thought how funny it would be if it had been my outspoken daughter-in-law.

# First Crush

No music was playing that day, but if there had been it would have been "You Send Me." and I would have swooned.

I was a thirteen-year-old romantic who went to the movies every Saturday and pretended falling in love with the leading man.

That Saturday had been different. I had seen this cute boy in the balcony and our eyes met. My friend nudged me and giggled.

Was he really looking at me? He couldn't be...he was one of the older boys. Yet every time I looked over, he was staring. At me! I couldn't believe it. What would I do if he said something?

Later, when I left early and went to the Ladies Room, I saw him get up too. He was hanging around outside the Ladies Room when I came out. As I walked up the hill towards home with the gang, I kept sneaking a peek back till I saw him. He was standing in front of the movie theater.

All these years later, I picture him in front of the movie theater, the marquee lit, as if spotlighting the hero in the movie. And as if in a movie, the other people fade into the background, until he stands alone, lighting a cigarette, head bent, blond hair falling into his eyes. Slowly he tosses the strand of hair out of his eyes. My friends are no longer around, and it is just the two of us—hero and heroine. I look at him, willing him to meet my gaze. In my memory he looks up and smiles.

Though Ernie gave me my first kiss, and I spent my adolescence having mad crushes on him off and on, Billy Rotunda was my first serious boyfriend. He was three years older than I was and a big influence on my life. Because I had very few rules and little structure in my home life, his influence was a lifesaver for me. He passed away at the age of 19 of leukemia.

# Spring Break 1959

For weeks my best friend Beth and I plotted to convince our parents to let me go with her on her family's annual spring trip to visit her aunts in Fort Lauderdale. Even though we had bought matching pink-and-white-stripe Bermuda shorts so we could look like sisters, no amount of begging, cajoling or sulking seemed to do any good.

They left shortly before Easter. I was heartbroken as only a fifteen-year-old can be, but resigned. Unbeknownst to me, Beth wasn't. Resignation wasn't her style. She dug her heels in and remained miserable until her parents relented.

The day before Easter she called, "Can you come? My mom and dad said it's okay."

I got off the phone and begged, "Please, please. I'll pay the airfare back from my allowance. I'll keep my room clean. I'll do anything. Please. Please." Finally, my mother gave in, called the airline and got me a seat on one of the new jet airplanes. It would take only two hours, instead of the four hours it took on a regular plane.

I had never been on an airliner, and here I was going all by myself. I wore my Easter outfit—a coral color "walking suit" that was all the rage that year, with its ¾-length jacket and straight skirt. Underneath it, I wore stockings and a garter belt. White gloves were folded on my lap. I felt so grown-up, like I was almost a different person...or about to be.

The stewardess, in her smart-looking navy-blue uniform, asked me if I wanted to hang the jacket up. I said no. It had been a crisp spring day when we left Idlewild Airport, and I couldn't conceive that it was actually going to be warm when we arrived in Florida two hours later, so I wanted it nearby.

I sat, butterflies in my stomach, waiting for this miracle to happen.

When we arrived, I stepped down the stairs onto the tarmac and into the glaring sunlight. I couldn't believe the heat, especially after the thirty-degree temps this morning in New York. I looked around at the other passengers as we headed for the terminal and saw they had shed some of their heavier clothing and were now in shorts and sleeveless blouses. I felt silly and overdressed in my heavy jacket.

As I neared the terminal, I saw Beth at the window waving to me. She, too, was in shorts, and a white summer blouse with a Peter pan collar. When I got inside, we hugged and jumped up and down with excitement.

We were staying with Beth's Aunt Rose, who had a house on a canal in Pompano Beach with something called a Florida Room. Later we all went to dinner at The Bahia Mar, which was right on the water. Sunshine, blue water and palm trees. It seemed like a dream.

The next day Beth's mom dropped us off near the beach in Fort Lauderdale, saying, "Now you girls be careful."

When the car was out of sight, we ran up to "the strip," where all the boys were. We were two girls: one with short blond curls, full lips and sexy figure; the other with long, thick dark hair, clear blue eyes and a shy smile. I wore a red knit Jantzen bathing suit with a blue and white V-neck; Beth wore a turquoise and white stripe two-piece suit. Both of us had one foot in innocence and the other itching for experience.

I looked down the street, past the family area, and saw a sea of teenagers on the beach—sitting, standing, dancing, sunbathing, walking. Hundreds and hundreds of kids. I had never seen so many in one place before. Cars cruised up and down the strip. Mobs of kids roamed in and out of shops, restaurants and bars.

They spilled onto the sidewalk, beer cans in their hands. Competing music was all around, from the bars and from transistor radios. The song "You've Got Personality," floated out of one bar. We mouthed the words in unison.

Our eyes met. Beth, mischievous and infectious, looked at me and smiled. What a week we were going to have, her eyes said.

The corners were full of kids shouting and whistling at the occupants of the cars passing by; the boys cruising slowly tried to entice girls to go for a ride with them. Convertibles were everywhere, boys hanging out of them, sitting up on top of the back seat. A few tourists drove by gaping at the goings-on.

A group of boys pulled over and rode alongside us. We pretended disinterest. "Where do you go to school?" one asked. "Where you from?"

After they pulled away, we regrouped. What were we going to say? We couldn't say we went to high school!

"Let's say we're sophomores at Hunter College," Beth suggested.

The next time we were ready.

"Want a ride?"

I was surprised when Beth quickly said, "Sure." But, then again, I was never quite prepared for anything Beth did. I was, however, a willing partner.

And so, the week started.

I liked the attention and followed Beth's lead, but most of the week I was on edge. She was much braver than I. We rode up and down the strip with a couple of fellas. A lot of guys were actually sleeping on the beach; we weren't interested in them. We did go on a date with two boys—one who went to a military school in Virginia, the other who went to Manhattan College. Both of them were from New York and had gone to Mt. St. Michael, our "brother" high school, so they seemed pretty safe.

When they took us back to Aunt Rose's and were saying good night at the front door, Aunt Rose swung the door open, almost knocking Beth over as she was about to kiss her date. We both giggled and went in.

On our last adventure, there were only two boys in the car and instead of just driving us up and down the strip like the other boys, they took us to a lonely beachfront.

"Hey, where are we going?" Beth asked. She was in the front with the guy who was driving.

"Too crowded back there. Let's go someplace more romantic."

Oh, my god, I thought—and more secluded. They probably wanted to "make out."

It was more secluded—off a dead-end road, empty up and down the beach and not another car in sight. But it wasn't long before they decided to take us back to the beach area, perhaps realizing that we were way too young and too inexperienced. Or they figured out that we weren't interested and decided to move on to greener pastures.

I was sure glad to be back in a crowd. Later that night, Beth and I were lying in bed in our baby doll pajamas. I whispered, "God, Beth, those last two guys. We could have been abducted or killed. That was scary—out on that deserted beach. No one even knew where we were."

But my words were lost on Beth. I looked over and she was sound asleep. If I knew her, she probably would have been dead asleep the minute her head hit the pillow.

If 1969 would become known as The Summer of Love, 1959 was The Spring of Where the Boys Are. The term "Spring Break" became popular and synonymous with Fort Lauderdale when the movie *Where the Boys Are* was released in the winter of 1960—and was forever immortalized in my mind with that vacation with my friend Beth.

# Barbizon Girl

High heels clicking on the pavement, I walk out of Grand Central Station, up two blocks toward the 42nd Street Library, turn the corner at 5th Avenue. Dozens of people jostle for space as I cross the street. Gray buildings tunnel my vision. Street hawkers shout, "Get your fresh hot bagel." The cacophony of sounds that is New York City—the car horns, the hot dog vendor, the guy selling bus tours, the buses heading crosstown—quicken my pulse, even though I have been making this trek from Yonkers to the city for the past three months—a mile walk from my house to the bus at the Yonkers/Bronx city line, then another bus by the Woodlawn Cemetery that took me to the NYC subway and eventually to the city.

In my high heels, nylons, white pleated skirt swishing around my knees, my brown hair in a flip, I pretend to be older than my seventeen years—more sophisticated. I hold my round white suitcase with pride—the suitcase that in 1961 in NYC says to the world, "I am a model," or in my case hope to be one.

I recall the day my friend Donna told me she was going to go to The Barbizon School of Modeling. "You're so attractive and thin, you should come with me," she said. I had never thought of doing anything like that. I knew people thought I was pretty, and I saw the way boys looked at me, but I never really felt pretty. But I kept thinking of what Donna said, and my mother said it would be good idea, would give me confidence.

Donna and I made the first trip together. When we got off the train at Grand Central, we were confused and disoriented—but excited. We finally found our way to the school. It was in a super ordinary building right off of 5th Avenue. A small entryway and an equally small elevator took us up to the second floor, where a bevy of chattering girls waited. A beautiful, long-legged receptionist took our names, and we sat down and waited for the big interview to get into the school.

At the orientation, the instructor explained that there are three kinds of models: full-time showroom models, seasonal models, and fashion models. The first made the least money but had the most longevity. The latter made the most money, but generally had the shortest career.

Last week I graduated, and I am officially a Barbizon Girl. I am here, today, for my first "lead"—actually two—and I hope to get a summer job as a model before starting my freshman year at City College of New York in the fall.

I think about the last three months: the interview, walking across the room, past those former models observing my every movement, taking my measurements: 34-24-37. Okay, I'd have to work on that hip measurement. One inch less should do it.

One week they taught me about make-up. I sat in front of one of the big make-up mirrors with the round-bulbed lights, and seasoned models taught me the tricks of the trade. Almay. Non-allergic. All the girls sat with their make-up cases and capes as the instructor demonstrated how to apply foundation, powder, lipstick, eye make-up.

"Take care of your skin," the instructor said, "It's one of the tools of your trade."

Another week I learned to glide across the room as a runway model. "It's not about you," they told us, "it's about the clothes. You are not there to swish and sway and call attention to yourself, but to be a mannequin." I tried to picture in my mind walking—pegged skirt, high heels—across the room, pivoting just so, as critical eyes judge my every move.

Then we learned diction. Correct pronunciation. Speak slowly, carefully. Practice, practice, practice. I got little booklets each week to reinforce the lessons. Each lesson a different color: pink, blue, green. Laminated orange Barbizon cards, emblazoned with their logo in black, were marked with the lesson learned, my weight, and measurements.

Now, as I wait for the elevator, I get a secret thrill knowing that those around me know I'm a Barbizon Girl. I go upstairs with some of the other girls and collect two leads for this week. One of the leads is across from Bryant Park, just a few blocks away. Great. Down the elevator, towards Bryant Park.

I find the building, go upstairs and wait for the interview. While I wait, I scan the black-and-white sketched ads on the wall that appear in the fashion section of the *New York Times*—Franklin Simon, Bergdorf Goodman, Saks Fifth Avenue. I'm called in, and there's a young guy, dressed in black, drawing at a sketchpad. He tells me to get up on a dais in front of a wall of floor-to-ceiling windows.

"Just get up on the platform. Move around. Pretend you're in an evening gown, dancing around and showing off, until I see something I want to sketch."

I walk over to the platform and step up. From there I can see the traffic on 42nd Street and people in Bryant Park. I get so caught up in the view that I forget he wants me to move around.

"Okay. You can move now," snaps me out of my reverie.

I start to move around but feel clumsy. Awkward. I don't know what he wants me to do, feel stupid pretending I have a gown on, but I turn this way and that, my arms up, down and around. Oh, god, I think, how am I supposed to do this? I try to imagine what those ads in the paper look like. But can't. Who knew this is how it is done. Nothing in modeling school has prepared me for this. On the contrary, this feels like it's more about me than about the clothes.

"That'll do," he says abruptly. "We'll call, if we need you."

I know they won't.

I look at the other lead. Rosgren's, 38th Street.

Waist cinched, head held high, I walk to 6th Avenue, then head south. On the way, I pass a construction site and hear some wolf whistles and catcalls. "Hey, babe, what ya doin' later?" "Va va voom." A blush of pleasure rises to my cheeks, while I pretend to ignore them. I can't help but smile, just a little bit.

I feel relieved to have that awful interview over. Hopefully the next one will be better.

Once I turn onto 38th Street, it is bedlam. Men pull and push racks of clothes. Some are running, some walking leisurely, one whistling. There are shouts, curses and friendly helloes. Lots of noise and congestion. The Garment District.

One guy is pulling two racks—one with each hand—with bolts of fabric in different colors and textures. If there isn't enough room for them to get through on the sidewalk, they wheel the racks into the street. One guy is hauling a naked mannequin across the street.

Three tall women walk abreast towards me—models, I'm sure, in their slim black dresses, high heels and tell-tale round cases. Guys ogle them.

I check the address again—230 West 38th Street.

Ooops, I was so busy looking at all the activity, I passed right by it. I double back, go in, take the elevator to Rosgren's on the second floor. I go to the receptionist and tell her I'm here for the modeling job. No wall of windows. No real waiting room. I stand and wait.

The manager comes out. He explains that the job is for a showroom model. They make coats. Buyers from various stores come in, look at coats to purchase for their stores. I would be expected to model the coats for them, and on occasion go into the back room where the head tailor would custom fit the coats to my figure.

He asks me to try on one of the coats and walk around the showroom. Now this is more like it. This is what they taught me to do at Barbizon. This is my kind of job. I glide across the room, make a few turns, show the features of the coat—the buttons, the collar, the pockets.

"Okay," he says, "give your information to Joyce. You can start on Monday."

I have my first modeling job. Yippee!

As it turned out, it was my last modeling job as well. For one summer I got a peek into the world of modeling. In truth, the best part of the job was the walk from the subway station to work each morning—in my high heels and the signature round white suitcase. The rest of it was pretty dull. The fittings by the older ethnic tailor who would smooth the cloth across my chest, and I would pretend not to notice because I didn't know how to handle it. The modeling in the showroom for the blasé middle-aged buyers from out of town. The boredom between showings. The day-to-day world of the showroom model was less than glamorous.

It was, though, the beginning of my life-long love of New York City. I thrived on its energy and excitement. I walked through the Garment District every day and breathed in the bustle and hustle. I loved the appreciative glances—and, yes, the wolf whistles. I savored this during that summer of 1961, before the feminist movement told us that this was demeaning.

That summer, however, I basked in the much-needed attention.

# ERNIE AND LYNN
## —STARTING OUT

# In the Beginning

In 1961, many girls got married right after high school, or if they were lucky enough to go to college, right after that. Monsignor McWeeney, in the yearbook, wrote a few words of advice to the graduates of my all-girls high school. He mentioned some of the paths our lives may take. We may become secretaries or teachers or nurses—not lawyers, professors or doctors. Even though our high school was difficult to get into and therefore had exceptionally bright young women, that seemed to be the acceptable choices for girls at that time.

Foreshadowing: But there were seismic changes rippling below the surface, without my realizing it. Betty Freidan's groundbreaking book, *The Feminine Mystique*, would come out in 1963. But that was still two years away, and it would take much longer for some of the changes foreshadowed in her book to reach mainstream America, even in progressive New York.

# Clash of Cultures

In every love story, the lovers can usually remember the moment they met. I wish I could remember the moment I met Ernie, but I don't. He was one of the boys in the neighborhood. We grew up together, played together, since we were about seven. I knew his family since I was a little girl.

His parents made a striking pair. I remember one time in particular: his mother wore high heels and a bright yellow sun dress with a bare back; his father wore white pants, white tight-fitting shirt and white shoes, his black hair slicked back. Little did I guess back then, even though I spent weeks at a time with mad crushes on Ernie, that I would one day marry their son.

There are fragments of memories: games of doctor and house played in Ernie's backyard, birthday parties, sleigh riding with Ernie down the hill in front of his house, the attic where Ernie took me to show me his trains, but it was sneaking a kiss that he was really interested in. We listened with guilty ears, afraid of getting caught by his seemingly ever-present mother.

Sometimes I would sit on the steps in front of Ernie's house dreamily listening to him play "Lady of Spain I Adore You," on his accordion, the music wafting from the window above. Ernie's grandmother, his father's mother, dressed in black and wearing old-lady shoes, would come out, broom in hand and begin to sweep the steps, ignoring me though there was no mistaking I was there. She started at the top of the steep stairway, thirty steps or so, in spite of the shy, lovesick girl sitting below. I would move before she got too close.

I had planned to leave the neighborhood far behind when I daydreamed of attending college in Bennington, Vermont, or Antioch, Ohio, or Amherst, Massachusetts. Instead, after a semester at City College in Manhattan, I found myself pregnant and following a different path.

Ernie and I were married on January 13, 1962, in a small hastily planned ceremony at Our Lady of Mt. Carmel Church in Mt. Vernon, where Ernie's mom and dad were married and where he was christened. My father wasn't told till shortly before the service for fear he would drink before we got there and embarrass me.

I wore a simple white wool dress and short veil. I did not walk down the aisle on my father's arm, but chose instead to enter from the sacristy. Though it wasn't as I had imagined, I was a happy bride.

There were two celebrations. My family had a boisterous gathering at the American Legion: lots of beer, cold cuts, potato salad, deviled eggs. Singing and kids running around. I think my grandmother even did the Irish jig. Ernie's mother and father came too. After that, Ernie and I spent the night at the Hilton Hotel in Tarrytown, which may not seem like much of a honeymoon, but was pretty memorable for me, especially the part when we checked in as Mr. and Mrs. Ernest DiGiacomo. I swelled with pride.

The next day when we got home from the hotel, Ernie's parents had a small quiet party for us at their house, just a few of Ernie's aunts and uncles, no kids. I saw right away why his mom wanted to have her own party. They had so much food, mostly Italian dishes, and fancy little pastries—and no liquor. It was all so refined compared to my family's get together.

That was the first day of my new life, in a new home. Hope and love filled my heart. Since we were only eighteen and couldn't afford our own place yet, I moved in with his extended Italian family. It was only two-and-a-half blocks from where I grew up, but it was a world away.

My home on Kimball Avenue was a one-story, asphalt-shingled house with a coal furnace. I was always cold in winter. One morning, as I sat shivering at the table eating breakfast, my feet on the chair, my quilted bathrobe wrapped around my legs, my grandmother said, "you'll never get a husband sitting like that."

I quickly answered, "I'll find a husband whose house isn't freezing."

We ate dinner in the dinette on a Formica-top table, hardly ever with a tablecloth, not even on a Sunday. The TV was usually on, which I hated. My grandmother did the cooking, which was bland and predictable—mashed potatoes, canned vegetables, and meat, usually ham. No seasoning was used, except salt and pepper.

There was never enough hot water; we had to heat enormous pots of water on the stove to take a bath, so it was a luxury. Most days we just took a scrub bath.

Their house was solid, made of brick. I had to climb two stories to the entryway; it made me see the world differently from that height. There was a formal living room twice the size of ours with a real fireplace.

One of the things I liked most was that the dining room set was real wood—I think it was mahogany—with carved legs and fancy carvings along the edge.

On Sundays, they all sat around that table, set with fancy dinnerware and glassware on a lace tablecloth. And everything matched. And the food! Rich and tasty, things I had never eaten before—chicken parmigiana, veal cutlets, string beans with garlic and red sauce and something called torta, stuffed with cheese and spinach. I had loved reading about families who lived like this.

Their home was full of breakables, not a single thing out of place, polished wood floors with area rugs, red velvet sofa with pillows placed just so—not like our house where we could jump on the sofa or the bed and where there were no wood floors or furniture you had to worry about scratching. I felt out of place. I didn't belong in a breakable world.

I was dazzled by the differences—real and imagined—between

his family and mine: the richness of the food, the apparent attraction between the mother and father, the protectiveness of the mother and grandmothers. This was the type of family and love that I longed for.

I was navigating unknown territory of a culturally different household. His Italian family and my Irish family were on opposite ends of the spectrum on just about everything, and I had no roadmap.

I never guessed the intrusiveness of such devotion into the private world I had created for myself.

Reading, which had always been my refuge, was looked at askance. If I left a book or magazine down for more than a few minutes, Ernie's mom would straighten the room and put it away. My father-in-law warned my husband, "She's too much with the books."

Their bathroom not only had a tub, but a shower as well—and there was always enough hot water. But when I was in the bathroom, my mother-in-law would say "do you need a towel?" or "do you have enough soap?"

She seemed to be always there. I know she meant well, but I didn't have enough time and private space to sort it all out. I was used to time alone to ponder things.

This kind of nurturing didn't feel like I thought it would, not like when Ernie would look in my eyes with his velvety brown ones and see me, the real me, and still love me.

I hadn't realized how much freedom I had to come and go as I pleased. Both my parents worked and in the evenings they would often go to the local bar and I was left to my own devices. I could be gone all day—and I often was—and they would barely notice or care. There were nights when the fighting at home was so loud that I would slip out of my bedroom window and roam the neighborhood. Alone. No one missed me.

I remembered whole days of doing nothing, walking for miles with my cousin and then deciding to ride the elevated train for the afternoon just for fun. I remembered reading for hours on end, getting lost in a book. I hadn't realized just how delicious it was to do that.

In their house, one grandmother lived next door, another upstairs; comings and goings were noticed.

There seemed to be no escape. There, nothing was shouted; clues were harder to decipher, yet seemingly vital. It was a subtle world of honeyed words that sometimes meant something else.

"I know how tired you must get, being pregnant. It's hard for you to get up on time in the morning," my mother-in-law would say. Did I get up too late? Was this meant to be a criticism? Or was it sincere? I never quite knew how to take things that were said. I began to realize that it wasn't okay to sleep late in this house, just as it wasn't okay to have breakfast in my bathrobe.

In the kitchen in the morning, she would make me anything I wanted. Eggs? Cereal? Pancakes? An eggnog?

"An eggnog?" I asked. Surprise lingered on my lips. The only eggnog I knew was the New Year's Eve kind with liquor in it.

Her face brightened. "Yes, I'll make you one. You'll love it. It'll be good for the baby too."

I watched as she pulled a glass container from the cupboard. She unscrewed the top, which had a handle you turned and a metal forklike thing underneath. She cracked two eggs into it, added some milk, vanilla, sugar and cinnamon. I watched, mesmerized. She spun and spun the handle until the mixture inside was frothy.

No one had ever taken such care of me before. It felt uncomfortable in a way.

She poured it into a glass. I drank it, and it was delicious. More like dessert than breakfast. And it was good for me . . . and the baby.

So, breakfast was over. Then what? Could I help with the dishes, I would ask. No, she'd say, she would do them.

Eager to learn, I watched my mother-in-law, copied what I saw, tried to practice being what I thought a housewife should be. My mother-in-law was generous with her advice and patience, but usually would end up doing it for me. She seemed reluctant to give me the reins. And after all it was her kitchen.

"Here, I'll do it.... Let me, it's easier.... Just go sit, I'll finish." So, I'd sit and feel useless.

One morning I eagerly said, "I'll go make the bed."

"Oh . . . oh, okay," she said with a hint of surprise in her voice.

From her tone, I guessed I should have made my bed before breakfast. I peeked into her room and saw their bed already made and the room as neat as a pin. I looked at our room, covers askew, a book on the night table, and some papers and a pen. Ugh.

Every day I would sit with my mother-in-law, often her mother or her mother-in-law, or both, around the kitchen table. As we sat, a wealth of things was delivered right to their door: fresh produce from the Italian vegetable guy in his lopsided truck every few days, the butcher delivery boy on his bike once or twice a week, the seltzer delivery once a month. The Dugan man delivered bread and fresh baked goods each morning that they would have with their coffee. And, of course, the milkman delivered milk.

My mother-in-law's mother, with her twinkling eyes and sweet smile, always made me feel she was on my side and understood how I felt. So much can be conveyed with just a knowing look. The other grandmother wasn't as friendly and often spoke only in Italian.

I found it hard to pretend to be interested in their conversation. My mind kept wandering to the book in the bedroom, wondering what happens next. My eyes glazed over as I looked at the intertwining design of the kitchen wallpaper, the round red clock....Tick...tick...tick...tick. I wanted to learn to be a housewife, to cook, but when I tried to help, I always seemed to do something wrong.

Ernie worked for his father, at his auto repair shop in the Bronx, six days a week with no set hours, often getting home quite late despite my pleas. I could not look forward to a specific time when he would arrive home. The days seemed endless. After a long day of work, dinner and after-dinner talk, there was hardly any time for us to talk or be alone.

At night I lay in bed listening for the pulse that beat below the surface. Sometimes I would overhear some of the things they said about me, and how they would misinterpret things I had said. It was strange not to be understood. I just couldn't seem to find the right things to say or do.

I just wanted to read my books; those I could understand.

And I didn't want to rock the boat.

I began to try to envision a life away from that house, a life on our own—an apartment, maybe one day a little house for our soon-to-be family. When I lived at home, I had a manila folder with pictures cut from magazines of rooms decorated the way I would like my dream home to be. I started to conjure up some of those pictures and think about what it would be like to have our own place.

Ernie didn't receive a salary per se: his father gave him what he needed. So, we really couldn't save money to get our own place but were dependent on them. I, however, was anxious to be on our own.

Ernie and I began to take Sunday drives through neighborhoods in Scarsdale and Hartsdale to look at houses we might one day be able to afford and try to picture ourselves living there.

"I like that front entry."

"How about that backyard? Isn't that pretty? That's what I'd like ours to look like."

Though it was mostly me making the comments, Ernie went along with it. He was more practical, thinking about how we would go about doing it. I'd come home gushing about my plans and hopes and dreams, knowing they were a long way off, but a possibility and something to aim for. But another overheard conversation brought me up short.

"She's taking him to see houses to show him ours isn't so special."

I was crushed. How could they think that? How could they

imagine I was the kind of person who would do that? Does the word "dream" even exist in the Italian language?

I crawled into bed with Ernie, nestling up against him for comfort. We shared what used to be Ernie and his brother's bedroom. Two single beds, one on either side of the room. I often snuck across the room and into the small bed with him.

Their house, seeming so large when I first moved in, started to feel smaller and smaller.

Teetering between two worlds: child and grown-up, single and married, Irish and Italian, I tiptoed softly and sometimes cried myself to sleep at night.

**Reflection:** Even today, I am hard-pressed to answer why I felt tethered to that house, unable to escape. The bars to the cage were mostly of my own making, though at the time, I didn't realize that. I viewed them as solid, immutable. The bars were my own insecurities and fear of their disapproval, but I believed that they had put them there.

And thinking about it now, I can understand how difficult it must have been for them too. In many ways they had opened up their arms, as well as their home, to me, and I and my parents must have seemed ungrateful.

My parents didn't do anything to lend a hand, expecting his parents to provide whatever I needed—doctor bills, dentist visits, things for the baby. They didn't even have us for dinner, and hardly ever called to see how we were. I'm sure they resented that, and with good reason. My mother-in-law had tried to be kind and generous, but I had been raised in such a different environment that I didn't always know how to respond, or my feelings got hurt too easily.

# A New Family

On June 16, 1962, Ernest Arthur DiGiacomo was born at St. Joseph's Hospital in Yonkers, and we became a family of three. We brought him home, glowing at this perfect little miracle, into the arms of his waiting grandmother, grandfather, plus two great-grandmothers and a great-grandfather.

We bought a fancy baby carriage, called a pram. It was green and white, with two large wire wheels and two smaller ones. Fit for a king. Ernie's mother gave me a beautiful, hand-crocheted coverlet, with light green satin underneath, that had been on his father's carriage. It was held in place by two silver prongs. I was thrilled to have something so beautiful and meaningful. I wanted the best for this child—nothing but the best.

Afternoons I would take the baby for a walk around the neighborhood, just to get a breath of fresh air—for both of us. I pushed that carriage so carefully up and down curbs that you would think it held the most perfect, delicately painted breakable egg, instead of a baby.

I read Dr. Spock and every child-rearing book I could find. I wanted to get this right.

# 138 Alexander Avenue

In September of '62, Ernie started to work for General Motors in Tarrytown, getting a real salary. I hoped this would change things, but no one seemed to be in any hurry, except me. Ernie and I started to look for an apartment, but Ernie seemed reluctant to change the status quo.

Finally, feeling smothered, I started looking on my own, determined to find a place for us. I did, when young Ernie was about one and a half. It was around the corner and halfway up the block from Ernie's parents.

It was an apartment on the first floor of what was meant to be a one-family house. The owners lived upstairs. There was a small kitchen with ugly royal blue tiles halfway up the wall and dark gray linoleum. There was only one bedroom. The biggest drawback was that the bathroom was downstairs in the basement.

I could see the potential, though, and it would be ours—all ours.

Our rent was $80 a month. The only other bill we had, besides our once-a-year car insurance, was our phone bill. If we wanted to make a large purchase, most stores allowed customers to pay "90 days cash." Ernie was making great money at GM—two dollars an hour—eighty dollars a week, sometimes more if he worked overtime.

I loved decorating that apartment. We covered the tiled walls with white contact paper, with a hint of blue and a fleur de lis pattern. We covered the floor with a white linoleum with a discreet turquoise pattern running through it. We put up a turquoise shelf to hang our new aluminum pots from. For a finishing touch, we put up a blue and white gingham fabric shade on the kitchen window. We hung a clothesline out that window.

I breathed easier in our own place, without feeling that other people were watching my every move. Now I could read all I wanted in my spare time.

In my eagerness, I got up at the crack of dawn to see my husband off to work, even though I wasn't a morning person. I packed his lunch in a metal lunchbox, often with little love notes inside—a surprise to put a smile on his face during the day.

I would clean and make the apartment sparkle. I would feed the baby, watch a little TV, then I would take little Ernie out for some fresh air. I would push the carriage down to McLean Avenue most days, meet the other mothers in the park near St. Barnabas and chat.

On rare occasions, we would walk up McLean Avenue to Sit 'n Chat for a bite to eat or something to drink. Then it was home to make dinner.

We were happy there.

# Love Nest

We lived in an apartment in Yonkers, New York, that had the bathroom in the basement. Ernie and I were only twenty then, so we could do that. There was no heat in that bathroom and on winter mornings, the toilet seat was bitter cold. But there was a clawfoot tub you could sink into up to your neck...almost. Fill it with bubbles, and you could practically float.

It was our first apartment, really meant to be the first floor of a two-story house. Our bedroom was where the living room was supposed to be—big and luxurious, with five large windows across the front. Ernie and I made custom shades from fancy sheets for those windows with a special fabric stiffener and shade kit. Ernie hung the shade—after we struggled ironing them, getting the pattern just right and stapling them to the rods—and I stood back and smiled. The cream shades with the burgundy design along the bottom, with sheer white curtains on either side, against the backdrop of burgundy walls looked straight out of a magazine.

The rent was $80 a month. Those were the days when you were told that your mortgage or rent should be one week's salary. At the $2 an hour Ernie was making and a forty-hour week, we were right on target.

There was a big double sink in the kitchen where I would wash the clothes and hang them out to dry on the clothesline, which hung out from the kitchen window and across the backyard. In the winter, if it got cold enough, the wash would stiffen like a board and I would have a hard time bringing it in, especially the towels. I remember the gleam of ice crystals on them as I tugged them in off the line. In summer, they had that crisp clean smell of early morning and sunshine.

I am not a morning person, but getting up at 4:30 and making Ernie breakfast before work during those first years of our marriage made me happy. I filled his lunch box while he got dressed, often tucking in a little love note—sometimes with silly invitations to romantic encounters later in the day.

What exuberance I had decorating on our meager budget. I combed through decorating magazines for ideas. The kitchen had old, ugly dark blue tiles halfway up, which I covered with pale blue contact paper with a fleur de lis pattern. Turquoise was *the* color in 1963. We put up shelves in the kitchen, painted turquoise. They held my shiny new aluminum pots with their turquoise lids. White linoleum with a turquoise pattern and a blue and white gingham shade were the finishing touches.

We couldn't afford a couch, so we had a twin bed in the living room that we covered with an olive-green tailored bedspread, so that it looked a bit like a couch. In that room we also had a small dining room set with a Danish modern "buffet," which was really a chest of drawers for baby Ernie.

It wasn't much when I look back on it now, but to me, then, it was a palace—my own domain.

Because we had lived with Ernie's parents when we first got married and didn't have our own place till our son, Ernie, was about a year and a half, we had never really lived alone together. So, once we got our own place, we couldn't keep our hands off each other. We were like a pot ready to boil over. But because we were so young, we had this strange feeling that we were playing house.

It sounds like a cliché to say life was simple then, but it was. Those three rooms were our love nest, where we dreamed of our future, but were content with our present.

# Daydreaming and the Sears Catalog

I remember the hats, especially the hats: hats with flowers and hats with feathers, with veils and without, available in beige, black, pink and lilac. I sat and surreptitiously stole a look at the Sears catalog. I could feel the thin black and white pages flip through my fingers. The year was 1963. We were at Aunt Jane and Uncle Bob's house in the family room of their hi-ranch. I soak up the atmosphere of the "normal" middle-class family. A family room! Who ever heard of a family room?

My baby was asleep in the car bed we had brought in from the car. Their four rambunctious youngsters, three boys and a girl, gave us a taste of what we had to look forward to. Their four-year-old girl was peeking in at the baby, while the three boys ran around the house and up and down the stairs. Aunt Jane and Uncle Bob remained unruffled.

While Aunt Jane and Uncle Bob were busy, I had a few precious minutes alone with the Sears catalog. I devoured it. Just reading the descriptions of each item was a pleasure. It was my doorway to daydreams. Daydreams of pretty hats and lacy white blouses. They had curtains and bedspreads, wallpaper and kitchen gadgets I never even knew existed.

This was before two-car families, so I had little opportunity to get out and shop. It was also a time when we, two twenty-year-olds, had little discretionary income. It was a time when I didn't even realize that I, too, could have a Sears catalog of my very own and have the luxury of daydreaming in my own home.

So, I looked forward to our Sunday drives up the Thruway in our '54 Ford, across the Tappan Zee Bridge, not only for the Sears catalog, but for the lifestyle and parenting Ernie's aunt and uncle modeled for us.

My parents had been too unavailable to be role-models. Ernie's parents, I soon found out, were the other extreme: over-protective and anxious.

Aunt Jane and Uncle Bob's home was warm, comfortable, welcoming. They were the kind of parents I wished to emulate. I soaked up whatever I could, with the added bonus of the Sears catalog.

# In It Together

It was 1963. We were twenty years old. The Civil Rights Movement was in full force; the Beatles had just released their first album; Betty Friedan's *The Feminine Mystique* had just begun what would be known as the Women's Movement.

These things were not on our minds, though, as we cruised down the New Jersey Turnpike. We held our breath at each toll booth, as the clutch chattered. Our '54 Ford was a remnant from our dating years—navy blue sedan with candy-apple red wheels that Ernie had painstakingly painted in the days before marriage and a baby came along. Now we prayed that car would make it to Atlantic City—150 miles away, three hours driving time, the farthest we had ventured from home together.

We had saved our money, gotten my mother-in-law to babysit and were going for the weekend—the first time we had been away since we were married a year and a half ago. A honeymoon of sorts since we had only had one night in a hotel in Tarrytown after we were married.

I had seen an advertisement for a lovely old hotel with a swimming pool on the roof. I imagined cozy rooms, a charming lobby and romantic ambience. I pictured us swimming in the pool under the stars and a full moon, music playing softly in the background.

We checked in and went to our room. There was nothing lovely or romantic about it—only old, as in seedy, as in worn-flat chenille bedspread with holes in it. I sat on the bed and cried. This was shabby, without the chic.

"Ernie, I can't do this! Please," I begged, "can we find another place?" Finally, my tears prevailed. We checked out and found a small motel up the block—not romantic, but not seedy either.

A bit of the bloom was off my vision of a romantic weekend, but I quickly sought to replace it. So off to the boardwalk and the beach we went. We had both vacationed here with our families, but we were giddy being there by ourselves. Ernie won a huge shaggy dog for me by hitting targets with a ball. I beamed; he was my boardwalk hero. I insisted on having a charcoal drawing done of Ernie—he was oh so handsome with his thick black wavy hair and chiseled features. It was an outrageous extravagance for us.

When we went to the beach, I attacked the waves as I usually did, fearlessly. I loved to ride them in, but usually had my lifeguard father nearby to rescue me if I got in trouble. I forgot that little detail as I got more and more courageous. With each swell I jumped, then found my footing. The rhythm of the waves and the sunlight egged me on.

"You're out too far, come back in," Ernie called to me.

"I'm okay. I'm okay."

But with the next swell, I failed to touch bottom.

I searched again and again for a foothold and tried to get back to shore. The ocean pulled me out farther and farther. My heart raced as I struggled more and more. Ernie tried to pull me in, but the more he tried the more we both were tugged out farther.

A lifeboat finally appeared, and I felt myself being pulled into the boat by rough strong hands. I shook from fright, the cold and embarrassment as the two lifeguards rowed me back to shore, leaving Ernie to fend for himself. My eyes swept the ocean for him, but I couldn't find him.

Back on the beach, people gathered around and stared as I frantically sought Ernie and his comforting embrace.

Where was he? After what seemed like an eternity, there he was. We quickly and wordlessly gathered our things and left.

Ernie was silent as we trudged back to the motel. I was annoyed and hurt that he wasn't more comforting after my ordeal. When we closed the door to the room, he collapsed on the bed and shook uncontrollably.

As we sat there, our arms around each other, I realized what a marriage really is: this hadn't been my ordeal, but ours. We were in it together.

# The End of Camelot

On November 22, 1963, Walter Cronkite's voice interrupted "As the World Turns" with a statement that President Kennedy had been shot in Dallas, Texas. I sat transfixed. The announcement of his death came shortly after. Solemnly, Cronkite came on air and told stunned Americans that their young, vibrant president had died. His voice cracking, he told America that "… President Kennedy died at 1 p.m. Central Standard Time, 2 o'clock Eastern Standard Time, some 38 minutes ago."

He took his glasses off and put them back on again several times. America watched as he tried to remain in control of his emotions in the most challenging of circumstances.

We watched as Lyndon Johnson was sworn in as president on Air Force One, his wife by his side. A stunned Jacqueline Kennedy, still in her blood-stained pink suit, stood by. Kennedy's body was returned to the White House, then to the Capitol for viewing.

That Monday, Americans were glued to the TV, watching the entire funeral procession from the U.S. Capitol to the White House then to St. Matthew's Cathedral. At the White House, the procession resumed on foot for roughly a mile, led by a stoic Jackie Kennedy and the president's brothers, Robert and Ted. Many of us have images in our collective memory of John-John saluting his father, unaware that it would be for the last time; Jackie walking out of the church with her two young children, one on each hand;

Kennedy's coffin arriving at Arlington National Cemetery—his final resting place.

Network coverage of this event and all that would follow was unprecedented. The networks rose to the challenge of this craving for all-day coverage. It seemed insatiable. It was the beginning of 24/7 news coverage.

The next day, emotions still welling up inside me, I walked to the park, hoping to share my grief with friends. We hugged, some cried, and we tried to make sense of such an unimaginable, senseless act. Many people on the avenue looked shell-shocked.

Kennedy's assassination was beyond comprehension in our world of 1963. Kennedy's time in office became known as Camelot, and it ended that day in Dallas, Texas. A generation lost their innocence.

**New Awareness:** Though most of my energy was still focused on my little world, I started to pay more attention to what was going on in the larger world. I had been totally unaware of anything going on in Vietnam or a war escalating there. A little over a year later, on March 8, 1965, two battalions of U.S. Marines went ashore on the beaches at Danang, the first U.S. troops to be involved—but not the last. I was, though unaware at the time, a little over one month pregnant.

# A New Little Brother

Randall Scott DiGicomo was born Oct. 24, 1965. At that time a five-day stay in the hospital was pretty standard, so I probably got home around the 28th. It was one of the happiest days of my life. I was bringing my son home to our own place, not my in-laws' house. I had read everything I could find on how to avoid sibling jealousy. I didn't want my sweet little Ernie to feel that we were paying too much attention to the baby and not enough to him.

We arranged for Ernie to take him over to his mother's while he picked me and the baby up at the hospital. It would give us a little time to fuss over the baby before little Ernie got there to meet his new little brother.

My mother-in-law made me a beautiful bassinette, and we placed little Randy in it and tried to take in this new little miracle that was ours. I hadn't had the opportunity to do this with little Ernie because there were so many other people in the household.

My mother-in-law came a short while later with young Ernie, and I can still picture him peering into the bassinette with love and wonder at seeing his little brother for the first time. It is such a sweet memory.

# Blackout

A little over a week later, on November 9, 1965, at 5:30, the electricity went out. I had just started making the formula for the baby. Ernie got a candle and I measured out the powder and then the boiled water. I was anxious, though, because on the package they had stressed how important it was to measure the amounts accurately and to sterilize everything—the bottles, the nipples, the plastic rings that go around the nipples, as well as the tongs for removing them from the boiling water. I had the bottles in the rack of the sterilization pot, but I would still have to remove them from the boiling water, which would be more challenging in the semi-dark.

We didn't think much of it, assuming it was just a temporary local thing until we got a phone call from Ernie's mother saying that they had lost power too and so had his father at work and others in the family. And since refrigeration was essential to keep the formula safe, that now became a concern if it should last long.

During the night we got to change a few diapers by candlelight.

By morning, to our relief, the power was back on and the refrigerator was still cold. When we listened to the News, everyone was talking about the Great Northeast Blackout.

# SEARCHING FOR HOME

# What Next?

Now that we had two little ones, we were outgrowing our apartment. Almost every Sunday we started our search for either a larger apartment or a house we could afford. It was discouraging. There was nothing affordable close by, so our search expanded to areas that were farther away.

One Sunday, we took a ride across the Hudson River to Rockland County after seeing an ad in the newspaper about a new development of attached houses being built. The minute I walked into the model, I knew that it was what I wanted. It was so modern and new, but the one feature that I loved most were the windows. There were three huge windows across the front of the kitchen, a wall of windows across the back of the living room, and a wall of windows across a huge master bedroom upstairs.

We picked out a lot and bought the house for $17,990. The builder worked with us, saying that the house cost $18,990 and that we had put down a $1200 down payment instead of the $200 we really did. We saved the rest of the money that was needed for the closing while the house was being built.

We went up to see the progress most Sundays. The foundation, the framing, the electrical wiring, the sheetrock, the exterior, the windows, and, finally, the kitchen cabinets. Towards the end, we found out what the house number was going to be—138 Halgren Crescent—the same number as our rental in Yonkers, surely a good omen. We had been happy in our little love nest.

# Village on the Green

We chose the lot in Village on the Green because it sat across from the park, right in the middle of the row of flat-roofed attached houses in Haverstraw, New York.

The year was 1966. Ernie and I were young marrieds with two sons—Ernie, 4, and Randy, a few months old. One weekend we drove about forty minutes north of where we grew up to look at houses.

It was love for me the minute I walked into the model and saw all the windows—back and front. And the newness of it all—bright, shiny, open, airy. Three bedrooms, 1½ baths. The green-and-white brochures showed patio homes encircling a four-acre park, neighbors gathered around a BBQ—a promise of friendliness, children playing, family, happiness.

After we made the purchase, I was excited each weekend when we drove up the Thruway, across the Tappan Zee Bridge and a half hour north to Haverstraw to see the builder's progress: foundation, bricks, floor, walls rising up before us.

I have a picture of our four-year-old in his Chesterfield coat and little fedora hat, walking through the partially finished house—two-by-four stud-framing separating the rooms —holding a rolled-up paper in his hands as if he were the architect inspecting his creation.

Each time I walked through the rooms, I decorated them in my mind's eye.

Our first real home together, and we were only twenty-three. The future was all before us—flawless, ideal. We would be free to live the way we wanted, without the encumbrance of Ernie's parents' interference and the stigma of my parents' alcoholism. Free.

# The Big Move

We moved in August, 1966. Randy was ten months old, little Ernie four and a half. Ernie and I were twenty-three. At that time, not many people moved out of our neighborhood. My mother's four sisters and one brother still lived in Yonkers. Ernie's parents were not happy with our decision to move so far away. We tried to explain that we couldn't afford anything closer, but I could tell that it didn't do anything to change their minds.

The house—a two-story townhouse, 1200 sq. ft.—was huge, compared to our little apartment. I was thrilled that I could flip a switch to turn on a light, instead of having to search for a cord to pull, especially in the dark. And not having to go to a laundromat was a real luxury.

We had very little furniture to fill the house and no money to buy more. In fact, when we bought the house, we couldn't afford all four appliances—refrigerator, washer, dryer, and dishwasher. My mother-in-law gave me great advice. She said, get the dishwasher not the dryer. You'll be sure to get the dryer, but if you don't get the dishwasher now, you might never get it. She was right.

The rooms were large, especially the living room, and looked cavernous and empty. We made a coffee table out of two decorative cement blocks and a piece of stained wood, but had no couch to put it in front of.

As it turned out, the GM plant where Ernie worked across the river in Tarrytown was working hours of overtime after we moved. He started working seven days a week, twelve hours a day. I hardly ever saw him. He'd come home, eat, and go to bed, but we got the dishwasher and then a couch and then... and then...

The only problem was we only had one car. By the time we got settled it was winter, and I knew no one. We were on a tight budget since moving and paying a $100 mortgage payment, house insurance, gas and electric, and phone bill. We had a limited phone plan and calls to Yonkers were billed as long-distance calls and were costly. They were cheaper if we called in the evening or on weekends, so we tried to do that, but it was during the day I needed someone to talk to. That winter was long and lonely.

The following year, I put my oldest on a school bus, followed the bus to the school and took pictures of him getting off the bus and walking into school for the first time. I had tears in my eyes. Now what? I turned to Randy my one-and-a-half-year-old and said, "What now?" He just laughed, as he usually did. It was just the two of us, and we now had a second car, so off we went.

I stood on the corner with the other ladies in the neighborhood, mornings and afternoons, waiting for the school bus. Sometimes I wore hip huggers, sometimes with my midriff showing. Once with a pair of go-go boots. Some of them had curlers in their hair and wore housedresses. Many of them were wives of police officers. I was younger than most of them. I had found a few like-minded people, but not many.

# Suburbia in the 60s

Winter, 1967

Our new home in Haverstraw, New York, was three times larger than our apartment in Yonkers, brand new and all ours! A washer and dryer in a cubbyhole off the kitchen—no more going to the laundromat. Lights with switches—no more grasping in the dark for elusive pull strings. It was a dream come true for me and Ernie— twenty-three years old and homeowners.

"Patio Living," the brochure had advertised. The brochure showed groups of neighbors gathered on a patio around a BBQ, eating, drinking and chatting—women in dresses with full skirts, men in slacks and open-collar shirts. A new concept in suburban living, the brochure said. Semi-attached homes around a four-acre park. Starting at $17,990.

Massive windows looked out onto our backyard where one day we hoped to build that patio the builders had advertised. A patio in the back and a park out front where the kids could play sounded like our idea of a friendly neighborhood. We would need that since it was all the way on the other side of the Hudson River from where we grew up in Yonkers—across the Tappan Zee Bridge.

We moved in August, had unpacked, made and hung up curtains, organized and stocked the kitchen. The furniture from our small apartment in Yonkers barely filled one-quarter of the living room; it was so empty you could almost hear an echo.

The excitement of Christmas had passed; the long winter loomed ahead, like the vast steppes of Russia. The cold weather was settling in, and I had no car. There was nowhere to walk with two little kids in tow, so the house was becoming a prison. A lovely prison, but a prison, nonetheless.

In Yonkers, even in winter I could walk the mile to the park near St. Barnabas and meet with friends and their kids. We would sit on the benches when the weather was nice, talk and watch as the kids played in the playground. On cooler days, we had walked our prams or strollers along McLean Avenue, sometimes stopping at Sit 'n Chat to have tea or an egg cream. Even in the coldest weather I had managed to get out and walk, if only to my mother-in-law's a block away.

In Yonkers, once a week, I played cards with the girls up the block.

In Yonkers, I could walk to the Cross County Center. Even though it was a three-mile trek, it had been an occasional treat for the kids and me on a beautiful day.

In Yonkers, it felt like home. I knew the streets, the houses, the people, even the slate and concrete sidewalks I had walked for over twenty years.

Now I roamed restlessly around my new home.

Little Ernie, four and a half, was lost in his own make-believe world, pushing toy cars over imaginary roads. A sweet, easy child, he was content; the baby, generally more rambunctious, was finally napping.

Another endless afternoon stretched before me. I picked up the mystery I was reading, read a few pages, and put it down. I just wasn't in the mood. It was a bit mindless, but it could endure the inevitable interruptions of two kids.

I wiped the countertop of my sparkling kitchen for the third time even though I had finished cleaning the house before lunch. Everything was brand new and didn't need much upkeep. I didn't even have to wash dishes now that I had a built-in dishwasher.

All of a sudden something the nuns used to say when I wore a fancy blouse to school popped into my head: All dressed up and nowhere to go. Well, I wasn't exactly dressed up, not yet anyway. I was still in my housedress, a brightly colored muumuu. Usually, I would change into something nice for Ernie's arrival home, which was on the dot of five. One of my favorite outfits was a fitted maroon turtleneck and gray bell-bottoms. I liked to look attractive for him when he got home from work. Besides it gave me something to look forward to.

He was usually tired and hungry. We'd have dinner, put the kids to bed, watch some TV, and go to sleep.

Then it would start all over again.

The winter months made it difficult to make friends until spring when mothers and children would emerge from their winter hibernation. We had met a few neighbors at a holiday get-together, but no one I could pick up a phone and call. Calls to friends and family in Yonkers were "long distance" and expensive, especially during day-time hours. Without a car, I was stranded.

I yearned for something to shake me out of my malaise.

The black-and-white TV constantly played in the background, but with only three stations, the choices were limited, mostly soap operas, which I had little interest in. The noise of adult voices, though, was somehow comforting. The drone of the TV was interrupted by a bugle-like horn; my heart began to race.

The Donut Man.

I would just get four—one for now and one for the three of us after dinner. I knew I shouldn't; I had already gained ten pounds since we moved here. I just couldn't help it. I could at least chat with The Donut Man, and if I was lucky, one of the neighbors might be out there too. I grabbed my jacket and ran outside.

"Two jelly, one custard—no, two custard, one jelly and an apple spice."

"Cold, isn't it!"

"Yeah, but at least it's sunny."

"Kinda slow today. Too cold. Nobody wants to come out."

"Well, maybe it'll be a bit warmer tomorrow."

"Hope so. See ya tomorrow."

"Well, maybe." Hopefully not, I thought. I really had to stop —the cost and the pounds were adding up.

I ran in the house.

"Hey, Ernie, honey, want some of Mommy's donut?"

By three o'clock I started to nibble on the second donut. Just a little bit, I thought. At four o'clock the phone rang. Who could that be? No one ever called during the day. I ran to answer it.

"Hello."

"Lynn?" a woman said. I didn't recognize her voice.

"Yes."

"I know you're new in the neighborhood. We have a social club that meets once a week. It's by invitation only and you and your husband were suggested by one of our members. Would you be interested?"

Wow, I thought, wow. "Sure," I said, my mind racing. Someone had recommended us. My body filled with a warm glow. "Sure."

"Well, we have a clubhouse in Stony Point that one of our members owns. We meet, as I said, once a week and party."

Immediately, I pictured getting a babysitter for the evening, getting dressed up to go out. Maybe I'd wear...

"At the end of the evening," she continued, "we throw our keys in together, then pick one out and see who we go home with."

"Ohhh." The glow turned to a blush, as awareness dawned, "Oh, well...aah...I'll have to ask my husband and...um...aah...and let you know, thanks."

I hung the phone up quickly, dropping it back on the receiver as if it were on fire.

Ernie came home an hour later. There were no donuts left.

# A Change
# is Gonna Come

In 1962, Helen Gurley Brown wrote and published *Sex and the Single Girl*, bringing female sexuality out of the closet. In 1965, she became editor of *Cosmopolitan*. Formerly a literary magazine, Brown reinvented it.

It was aimed at young single women, but many housewives ate it up too. The magazine was frowned on by many feminists; in it Brown advocated for women to have the sexual freedom that men already had.

Gloria Steinem went undercover as a Playboy Bunny at the Playboy Club in New York. She wrote an expose, published in 1963 as "A Bunny's Tale," in which she detailed how women were treated at those clubs. In 1969, Steinem published an article, "After Black Power, Women's Liberation."

The ground was shifting, and I could feel it. She campaigned for the Equal Rights Amendment, testifying before the Senate Judiciary Committee in its favor in 1970. She became the face of feminism. She wore jeans. She had long hair. She was a decade older, but I looked at her as a contemporary. I thought wow.

Outspoken Bella Abzug, in 1970, challenged the fourteen-year incumbent in the Democratic primary for a congressional district in Manhattan. She won and was a member of the U.S. House of Representatives from New York from 1971-77. She was a supporter of civil rights, including gay rights, and a strong opponent of the war in Vietnam. Known for her flamboyant hats, she once stated, "It's what's under the hat that counts!"

"The times they are a changin' "

My neighbor Vivienne up the block went to school to become a nurse. Another neighbor, Dorothy, rode around in her white Mustang convertible and enrolled in Rockland Community College. She challenged me to do the same. A new neighbor, Paula, moved in and I was awestruck. She wore jeans like Gloria Steinem, was outspoken and flamboyant like Bella Abzug. She was smart, hip and independent. I bought a pair of jeans, a mauve faux suede midi-coat and a knit hat that had a flower on the side and came down over my forehead. I was ready.

I was starved for intellectual stimulation. I read voraciously and joined a book group, but it wasn't enough. Then one day in April of 1970, as I was switching channels on the TV, through all the inane soap operas, I suddenly came across a man in a suit talking to a wild-haired young guy in a tie-dyed shirt who was ranting about Vietnam. Though he was obnoxious, sarcastic and rude, the show gave me something to think about. *The Phil Donahue Show* became a highlight of my weekdays. He had timely and sometimes controversial guests. Thoughtful questions from the audience and on the phone were like meat to a starving lion. I ate it up.

A friend of mine invited me to a Consciousness-raising Group. It was in an apartment of a friend of hers. We sat around in a circle in her dimly lit living room. We introduced ourselves and told the group a little about our backgrounds and why we were there. I said that I was a wife and a mother and felt vaguely like I wanted something more. Some of them were divorced or thinking of it. I went to a few sessions, but felt it wasn't for me.

Many of the women were with men who were not supportive. Ernie always encouraged me and supported me; that's the kind of relationship we had. When he dreamed of being a pilot, I opened a secret bank account for him and put aside small amounts each week until there was enough for him to take a few lessons. I knew that he would do the same for me.

# The 60s

The 60s is a decade that started out with a man walking on the moon, but ended with bitter protests and dissent that would divide a nation that had started the decade in Kennedy's Camelot.

Love beads and bell bottoms, bare midriffs and long hair. And freedom. We thought we were breaking the sound barrier. We thought we were the first generation to do so.

We believed in possibility. The possibility of a better world. The possibility of peace. The possibility of love.

It was a time when the youth of America felt themselves to be on the brink of history—a seismic event, the land shifting, opening up, and those witnessing not knowing just how the land would settle when it was all over.

Nineteen-sixty-nine was the epicenter of the event—The Summer of Love, of Woodstock, of high hopes and aspirations, of peace and love. John and Yoko recorded the historic, "Give Peace a Chance." The Stonewall Riots in New York marked the start of the Gay Rights Movement. Black Pride and the Civil Right Movement were strong.

It was an exciting intellectual, cultural and political moment in history. If you were young and idealistic, you believed that you could change the world.

And we were idealistic. We saw a need to protect our environment. The first Earth Day was in 1970. It led to the creation of the EPA, recycling and the Clean Water Act. The 26th Amendment of 1971, changing the age to vote to 18, had its roots in the 60s, when the anti-war activists shouted, "old enough to die, old enough to vote."

And night after night on TV, I watched the innocent faces of the young soldiers that were killed in Vietnam, like Christians being thrown to the lions, their lives cut short by decisions made by bureaucrats in Washington. My heart broke for them and their families.

Feeling somewhat impotent, I stood on the fringes of a few peace marches and envied those who could fully participate. I wanted the kids to know, even at four and seven, how important it was to stand up for something you believed in.

At the age of 26, I felt the tug of youth—the music, the political climate. We had thought about going to Woodstock, and after all these years I still have the brochure, with its purple and white graphic proclaiming "three days of peace and love," tucked away somewhere. Ernie's remark when he saw the rain and the traffic on the thruway was, "See it's a good thing we didn't go."

Me, I wasn't so sure. There I was again standing, watching on the sideline, wanting to be part of something. But I did feel the equal or stronger reality of grown-up obligations of a wife and mother of two.

It was still a year or two before I would go back to college and write commentary in the school newspaper.

It was before I figured out that my pen could do my picketing for me.

# Dream Deferred

I had a dream of going to college. In my junior year of high school, I pored over college catalogs and brochures. Two schools captured my imagination: Antioch College in Ohio and Bennington College in Vermont. I longed to get away from a troubling family situation, and they both had innovative programs that appealed to me.

As the time for filling out applications came, I realized Antioch and Bennington were more dream than reality. My full Regents scholarship would only cover schools in New York State. And even if I received a scholarship from those schools, my father didn't believe in women's education and refused to pay for the room and board that would be required.

I settled for City College of New York, or CCNY. I say settled, but once on the grounds of CCNY, located in the heart of Harlem, I couldn't have been more excited. With its stone Gothic buildings and atmosphere of intellectualism, it was everything I thought a college should be. The only flaw was that I had to go home to a disruptive household that made studying and concentrating on homework difficult; my father seemed determined to undermine my dream.

Ernie, my boyfriend at the time, was supportive though— picking me up at the train station when I had late classes. He wasn't going to college, but thought it was cool that I was. I almost had one semester under my belt when I found out I was pregnant. Ernie and I were married in January, right after the semester ended. We were only eighteen, so we moved in with his parents.

I did not sign up for the spring semester, but intended to return after the baby was born. I filled out all the forms to put my scholarship on hold.

My baby was born in June and I planned on going back to college in September. When I held my son in my arms, though, I realized how hard it would be to do that. Also, Ernie's mother, though she was loving and helpful (sometimes too helpful), felt like a threat. I feared that if I went to school, she might become more mother to my son than grandmother.

Still, I dreamed, but deferred my dream.

At twenty-two, I found myself pregnant with our second child. We were outgrowing our small three-room apartment one block away from his parents. Ernie was making good money at General Motors, and we had saved a bit, so we started looking for a house. We had to look farther afield to find something we could afford; Westchester was too pricey for us.

We finally found a community of attached townhouses set around a park about forty minutes upstate.

Still, I dreamed that someday down the road I might go back to school.

In the fall of 1966, we moved. Now with a house and two little boys to care for, my dream of an education was again put on hold.

Still, I dreamed, and read voraciously.

On a September day in 1970, I waved my youngest son off on the school bus. It was a time when women's liberation was being talked about. I had a loving husband who always encouraged me to be my best and to follow my dreams. We finally had a second family car, which made things possible. I found myself thinking of an education more earnestly.

I browsed through the Rockland Community College catalog I had picked up and felt an adrenaline rush unlike anything I had felt in a long time. Could I?

I had always intended to go back after I had given up my scholarship to be a full-time mom, but the reality of it seemed daunting.

Finally, I bit the bullet and signed up for English 101—Lanny Taylor, instructor. A river of doubt ran through me as I stood at the door of the classroom on that first day. Twenty-seven years old and I felt like a thirteen-year-old on my first day of high school. Worse, I felt like a gray-haired old lady trying to be one of those cute little hip-swaying nymphets in mini-skirts—all those bright, shiny faces. Dressed in matching slacks and top, I couldn't stand out any more if I had "married housewife with two children" written on my forehead.

I should try to channel my neighbor Dotty, who drove around in her white Mustang convertible and had gone back to school last semester, then I could do it. Just open the door and pretend. I straightened my back, walked in and pretended, like I had as a kid when I would "whistle a happy tune" and no one would ever know I was afraid. I felt the door glide open, then close behind me and the space between me and the nearest desk disappear. I was sitting in a college classroom waiting for the instructor and the next chapter of my life to unfold.

I found that I was bright and eager to learn—oh, so eager.

My dream of an education was beginning.

# Finding My Niche

Nineteen-seventy was a pivotal year for me. I had attended one semester of college after high school, going to CCNY with the help of a full Regents Scholarship. I gave up that scholarship, feeling that being a mother was more important at the time. I never regretted that decision, but I did regret not finishing college. So, with Ernie's full support, I signed up for my first course at Rockland Community College (RCC). It was two days a week while the kids were in school, and I was beyond excited.

Lanny Taylor's class was stimulating and challenging. I ate the books; I couldn't get enough. I was ravenously hungry with intellectual curiosity and made a pig of myself—trying to eat every morsel of knowledge I could.

It was the early 70s. The time was ripe—for me and the youth in America. The school was churning with change. The next semester I signed up for two classes, and I was lucky to stumble onto Reamy Jansen's journalism class. He was faculty adviser for the student newspaper and loved my writing. He encouraged me to get involved with the school paper, *Outlook*.

The newspaper throbbed with the conviction that we could change the world. We wrote about relevant, sometimes controversial, topics: Vietnam, Nuclear Power, Earth Day, Zero Population Growth, Ralph Nader and Product Safety, Women's Equality. I connected with this time and this place and these young people, maybe more that I had with the 50s and the all-girl Catholic High School I had attended.

The beat of the music of "Come Together," "I Just Can't Help Believin'," and "Aquarius/Let the Sun Shine In" vibrated through those heady days and I wanted to stay there forever—right in that moment, that time. I became News Editor, then Associate Editor.

I especially liked the camaraderie of the staff when we would stay late into the night doing the layout for the next edition. The adrenaline rush of it. Arranging the stories on the page, choosing the artwork, cutting some of the articles down to make them fit. It was like a puzzle. Then the relief when it's done—and ordering the pizza, patting ourselves on the back and thinking of the next issue. I loved the cycle of it, the rise and fall. The feeling that we were doing something important.

The spotlight I received because of my articles made the other teachers at the school notice me. I got inducted into the honor society and received an award named for a long-time professor, Henry Larom.

I maintained a 4.0 average, graduated summa cum laude. I was asked to be valedictorian, but because of a month-long cross-country trip we had already planned, I was unable to do it.

I had found my niche at an exciting time in history.

After graduation from Rockland, I went on to a four-year college: Ramapo College in New Jersey. There I finished my B.A. in American Literature, magna cum laude. At Ramapo I worked on the school's literary magazine—*Trillium.*

My dream of an education was complete. My life-long love of literature—both reading and writing—had begun.

# Yearning for Home

*"Home is a name, a word;*
*it is a strong one;*
*stronger than magician ever spoke,*
*or spirit answered to, in strongest conjuration."*
—Charles Dickens

The house at the top of the hill on Kimball Avenue is abandoned now—its contents left for junk. The electricity is turned off. Daylight wanes. The air is crisp and overcast on this January day in 1977. The winter chill touches something in me, besides the cold.

I walk into the house through the side door, as I had a thousand times before. This house had been "home" for the first eighteen years of my life. Now the empty house seems eerie, the walls silent. I find no welcome as I step into the kitchen, no warmth. Instead, I am assaulted by memories.

Memories—the word often conjures up something happy. A family. Laughter perhaps. Mostly for me it is angry words...slurred words...curse words. The voices echo off these walls. Images flash through my mind. The stale smell of the small house transports me back to a past I don't want to revisit.

It's the first time I have been back since Nonie died five months ago. My mother has remarried and has no interest in the life she had here with us. Now, the house is to be cleared out and sold.

You would think I would have no interest either, but somewhere within me I yearn...for something.

Looking to my right I see the dinette, where my father often sat after work with a beer and a cigarette in his nicotine-stained fingers. Meals were taken, often in silence or to the drone of the TV. The far window that opened to the backyard is where my grandmother hung laundry on the clothesline, summer and winter.

If I could wipe off the unpleasant memories, as one wipes the dust off a table, I might remember family gatherings in this tiny room—my grandmother's birthdays, Christmas get-togethers—old-time songs sung while my father played his harmonica or crooned a melancholy tune, the house filled with aunts, uncles, cousins. But, sadly, the dirt and grime of my unhappy memories mire my mind so that I am often unable to see beyond them.

To the left, off the kitchen, is where my bedroom was. I hesitate to continue. These walls haunt me. I think of the many nights I lie in bed, tired but unable to sleep until the anger and shouting stopped. Afraid. Afraid of what might happen if I fell asleep, as if I had some control over it. I always felt I had to do something to make things better, to make things right. Even now I feel that burden.

I close my eyes and can see my teenage self, squirreled away in my room, lost in the pages of a book, imagining myself somewhere else. Literature led me down many roads and showed me many different kinds of families and lifestyles.

My life outside my home offered others. My best friend and her Italian family added richness to the vision of my someday home. I still remember the first time I saw their pantry. Such abundance. I didn't even know there was such a thing as a pantry—a room just for food, shelves upon shelves of food. Our kitchen was sparse.

The home of my parents' friends Hazel and Bill added yet another dimension—art and culture. Bill was an artist and had walls filled floor-to-ceiling with artwork. Such a contrast to other 50s homes.

Church offered sanctuary when I needed it. The library offered escape, possibilities, companionship, choices, blueprints to different ways of being.

To capture my dreams and hopes, I assembled pictures of my dream home in a manila folder, carefully cut out of magazines. There was a kitchen with all the modern conveniences, a vividly purple bedroom, and a room lined with books. The home I longed for would offer small indulgences: a comfortable chair that invites you to read or reflect, a bed that embraces and relaxes, a bath that pampers and soothes the troubles of the day, a palette that pleases, a table that invites you to imbibe and savor. There should be objects of beauty that inspire or tickle the mind with memories and enjoyable thoughts, order that comforts amidst the disorder of the world outside.

I often wonder what happened to those pictures that sustained me and my hopes for a better place to be—a place that mattered and felt like home.

I turn away from these thoughts and face the reality of my mission. Fighting the clock and the impending darkness, I go into the living room where workers have piled things to be removed tomorrow morning. This is my last chance to retrieve something from my past. I rummage through the heap of rubbish—almost as tall as I am. Searching for something, I'm not sure what.

One day. Only one day to go through all this. I feel frantic. There is a fierce desperation in my search as I weed through one useless thing after another: keys to unknown doors, worn slippers, advertisements of long-ago sales. Junk. Mostly junk. Meaningless. Worthless.

I have my coat on, but still feel cold and sense again the evening coming too soon, the light fading from the room. Then my hand rests on a menu from the Queen Mary, with a date: June 1948. Memories flood back. A birthday not attended by my grandmother. A whole summer without her while she was in Scotland. I remember seeing a picture of her holding another little girl's hand. I find myself immersed in feelings of sadness of that five-year-old girl going on a ferry across the Hudson with her aunts and cousins, but no Nonie there like she usually was.

Finding the menu just propels me on. I rummage further and find an old insurance book of my grandmother's. Twenty-five cents a month checked off as PAID.

Again, I am thrust into the past. I can picture myself at the table with my grandmother and the insurance salesman. I recall the salesman, with his coiffed, steel-gray hair, wearing a suit. My grandmother would take out her coin purse and pay him, and he would mark it off ceremoniously. My grandmother was not given to idle chatter or inviting neighbors over for a cup of tea. A foolish waste of time she would have thought, but this was business, so she offered him a cup of tea and they would sit and chat for a while.

I shiver, from the cold and the memories.

Darker still...and colder, I plunge into the pile more rapidly. Throwing aside anything I think is unimportant, hoping for more treasures. Like gold to a prospector, I find a box of photos. Then I spy ledgers and bills from when my grandfather built the house on the lot behind our house. His cursive handwriting is splayed across the page. It gives me renewed energy to plod on and find something else.

Time to leave, I think, when a glint of chrome amidst the rubble catches my eye. I hold my breath and unearth it. It's the sugar bowl that always sat on our dinette table. Dented and with the top missing, it is a remnant of my past. It conjures up all the times my grandmother had tea at that table, times when we watched Loretta Young or Kate Smith or *As the World Turns*. But it's missing its top and it's all dented. With a sense of sadness, I leave it behind and call it a day.

I close the door firmly behind me, the wooden screen door resounding—wood upon wood—for the last time.

My eyes scan the yard. Outside the house is where my pleasant memories are. Memories of climbing the tree in the front corner, lying and daydreaming in the lap of the tree created where three large branches came together. Or hanging—free—from its limb by my knees. Off the patio, there's what's left of the brick barbeque my father built and cooked on for family picnics in the yard.

I loved seeing the peonies in bloom and the violets. I can almost see the tea rose bush I planted with my mother. In the summer I would pick up the peaches in the yard or from the tree, hard inedible fruit that Nonie would stew and tease the sweetness from. The rich aroma would rise from the pot and fill the kitchen. One of my favorite memories is my cousin Pinky and I lying in the hammock and rocking the summer day away.

I am exhausted, but the ride home gives me time to reflect. I begin to realize that I left the house, not only with a few keepsakes—the menu from the Queen Mary, my grandfather's ledgers, some photos, the insurance booklet, and a few other things—but I have come away with something more precious than possessions. I realize that what makes a home is love. I have that. I have two young sons whom I love beyond measure, and a husband who is the love of my life. So, I drive farther from that home I grew up in that never felt like home to me, and toward that place I have been yearning for. I have explored, searched, and found it. It has been there all this time, right there in the arms of my love, Ernie.

I am home.

# Taking Care
# of Business

Ernie had spent the week in Detroit on a business trip and I was meeting him at The Marriott in Tarrytown. As if we were lovers. As if this were a rendezvous.

Even though we had been married seventeen years, I felt the excitement, the anticipation, as I waited in the lobby. We had never really been apart, except for the two times I'd been in the hospital giving birth to our two sons. We would have a drink in the hotel bar before we headed home. He would tell me about his week, his trip.

I had dressed carefully for this 'date.' I wore a mauve faux suede midi-coat, my knee peeking out between the mini-skirt  and brown suede boots I wore. My long brown hair flowed to mid-back from under a rust-colored cloche hat, with a knitted flower on the side. I felt good, and I knew that Ernie would appreciate how I looked.

Finally, the airport bus arrived and he got off with a few of his colleagues, his briefcase in hand. Looking at him with his co-workers, I imagined not knowing him and meeting for the first time tonight. Not as the young boy I had grown up with, who gave me my first kiss, the guy I married at eighteen, but as the cute guy getting off the bus tonight. I looked at him with his thick dark hair, angular features, slim build and broad shoulders, and I wondered how a woman who met him for the first time —without knowing that boy I knew—would see him, what she would think of him. It made me look of him just a little differently.

Ernie came into the hotel lobby and looked at me, and I saw his deep brown eyes light up. He gave me a quick embrace and introduced me to some of the guys I didn't know. After they left to go home, we walked down a well-lit carpeted corridor to the bar area. We could hear the noise of the bar as we approached: music, laughter, noisy conversation.

Our eyes had to adjust to the dim lights. People were lingering around the bar, vying for drinks and attention, but along the periphery of the bar were two deep purple cushioned chairs with a small table between them. They were empty. We looked at each other, nodded knowingly, and headed straight for them.

We ordered drinks and settled in. In the background, "Taking Care of Business" played. Ernie sang along and squeezed me a little closer. I tingled.

After several minutes' conversation, I looked up and recognized our old friend Johnny sidled up to the bar, one foot up on the foot rail, elbow leaning against the bar. I was just about to raise my hand and wave when I noticed that his only-Johnny half-crooked smile was directed at a beautiful blonde next to him. In disbelief I watched as they laughed, then nuzzled up to one another.

You see Johnny and Marie, high-school sweethearts like Ernie and I, had been married the year before us and had always seemed perfect together. And that was *not* Marie. These thoughts passed rapidly through my mind as I continued to gaze, wondering what to do. Just then Johnny looked up, met my gaze, but like a stranger or an actor pretending to be a stranger, showed no sign of recognition. He looked away. I looked away.

I whispered to Ernie, "Johnny's over there with some woman. Let's get out of here." We quickly finished our drinks and asked for the bill.

On the way home in our old blue VW bug, we talked about

what had happened. To tell or not to tell Marie. We decided not to, but it was lost in the pent-up passion that crackled between us.

When "Night Moves" started to play on the radio, we forgot about Johnny and Marie and started humming along. Nineteen sixty-two was the year we got married.

We pulled off 9W into a parking lot overlooking the Hudson. It was one of those turn-offs frequented by those much younger than we were, but we knew the kids and the babysitter were waiting at home.

We caught up just a bit on our own night moves in that little VW bug.

# Looking Back

*"Wings are like dreams. Before each flight,
a bird takes a small jump, a leap of faith,
believing that its wings will work.
That jump can only be made with rock solid feet."*
—J.R. Rim

We lived in Village on the Green for thirteen years. Memories flash before me of those years. I see a young couple moving in, with a ten-month-old baby and a four-year-old. I see the husband working twelve-hour days, six and seven days a week, in order to furnish their first home. I see a wife poring over decorating magazines, and so appreciative of her husband's hard work that she has home-cooked meals ready when he gets home and makes sure he gets his sleep without the kids waking him.

I see the wife in this one-car family struggling with the reality of living far away from family and friends, but eventually meeting neighbors and going to neighborhood parties, but they always seem to enjoy their time together the most. I see yearly Halloween gatherings in the park with homemade costumes—one year their boys dressed like a mummy wrapped in strips of white sheeting and the other as a tin man made of boxes covered in aluminum foil. Kids in the neighborhood always got excited, wondering who would win best costume.

I see their oldest, then their youngest, boarding the bus for school, and the mother waiting at the school bus stop for their return, day after day, year after year. I see the young mother having play dates—before she or anyone had ever heard of play dates—with her friend Irene up the block and her two boys.

I see many Christmases in that house: the boys waking their parents, who then went downstairs and lit the tree while the kids waited at the top of the stairs—eager and excited. I see the looks of surprise and delight on the boys' faces as they come down and see the tree lit up and their toys beneath it.

I see the eager twenty-seven-year-old freshman mom heading off to the local community college when her youngest boards that school bus. I see this same mother discover a sense of herself —finding that she does well in school, is stimulated by it, joins the editorial staff of the school newspaper and writes columns for it. She finds she is passionate about the issues of the era, writes articles about them. In all her endeavors, she is encouraged by her husband.

I see her husband do well too at his job with GM—promotion after promotion. He travels to Detroit on a special project, and she is so proud of him. They have their problems too, like any other young couple making their way, but they manage to iron them out. I see one memory that always will bring a smile to her face and remind her of his love: she is upstairs and hears a lot of noise downstairs. He calls her down and she can't believe what she sees. There, sitting in her own kitchen, is the oak sideboard buffet that she had seen and loved in a store in Nyack. He had bought it, brought it home and surprised her.

I see them buy a gold Ford van that he fixes up for camping: a table and bench seats that fold down to a bed, a cabinet on the door that folds down for preparing and cooking meals. With its 60s era tie-dye curtains, shag rug and peace sign, they travel with the kids any chance they get, including a month-long cross-country trip when the boys are thirteen and ten.

She is outgrowing the neighborhood, ready for change, longs to live in a charming old house in Nyack, an artsy community just south of them along the Hudson River. He is leery, doesn't like change. I see them argue, look for houses; he finds something wrong with each of them. She goes to work, partly to prove they can afford the move. She wants something more; he is content. They finally find a house, with charm and character, in Nyack, twenty minutes away—an easier commute for him and it has a two-plus car garage that he loves. This chapter in their lives is drawing to a close.

Looking back at our time in Village on the Green, it seems like another lifetime, another couple. The move to Nyack was a positive one for our family. Young Ernie was a senior in high school, and because I didn't want him to miss graduating with all his friends, I drove him the twenty minutes each day to school and back. The school in Nyack was a much better environment for our youngest, Randy, who was just finishing his freshman year. It was a smaller school and he thrived in it. Because we had made one change, it made it easier for us to make others—all positive. The years we spent in Village on the Green were good ones and gave us a firm foundation for our future.

We had gathered memories, spread our wings, and moved on.

# Hiding Out
at the Library

The Yonkers Public Library in Getty Square—I look up. The stairs are high and there are lots of them. I hold my mother's hand tight. I can feel my banana curls bounce as I climb the high steps to the door of the library. My mother opens it, and I look up at the high, high ceiling in the big round room. My mouth opens in surprise when I look inside and see all the books.

My mother lets go of my hand and I wander over to shelves and shelves of books. I look up and up and up. More books than I've ever seen in my whole life. At home there is a phone table next to a chair in the living room with two shelves and three or four books on each shelf.

Who is going to read all these books? How long would it take me to read all these books?

"Mommy, Mommy, look."

"Ssh! Ssh!" the lady at the desk says. Like in a church, you had to be quiet.

I didn't know it at the time, but this was my first visit to a Carnegie library. *

At school, there was a small library at the back on the second floor. I remember being scared of the librarians there. They seemed formidable and ever present—watching and lurking like library police. We would be allowed in, a few at a time, and told to make our choices quickly. No lingering. We would go to the desk with one or two books. The librarian would take the card out of the pocket at the back of the book and mark it with the date it was due.

The first library that I went to by myself with my friends and where I had my very own library card was a small storefront in Woodlawn. Because it was in an old store, the wood floors were creaky and it was small, with the children's section all the way in the back. But my friends and I were more interested in the reference section where we could surreptitiously look for answers to questions we didn't know how to ask—about "childbirth," "pregnancy," "the curse," "breasts," and "penises." One of the librarians would sneak up behind us and ask what we were doing or if we needed help. We giggled, out of fear and embarrassment.

I was often told that I should be in the children's section, not the adult's when my inquisitive eye led me there. I loved the feel of the books, their pages, the excitement I felt when I discovered one that led me into a world I had never explored or when I met a character I adored.

After I got married and had my own children, I had the pleasure of taking my sons to the library, hoping that they would love reading as much as I did.

Later, when they were grown and we moved to Nyack, I dis-covered another Carnegie library.

Have you ever thought about your dream job? I hadn't, but I found one quite by accident.

I became active in The Friends of the Nyacks, a group interested in the architecture and the history of our unique community on the banks of the Hudson River. I gave walking tours, served as their secretary and president, and did their newsletter. I especially loved doing the newsletter. It reminded me of the days back in college when I worked on the school newspaper, *Outlook*.

When the Program Director of the Nyack Library quit, some-one suggested I would make a good replacement because of my work with The Friends organization. I was asked if I would be interested. One of the duties of the Program Director was to do the monthly library newsletter. Would I be interested? Of course, I would. I had never imagined such a position. To do a monthly newsletter *and* work in a library. A Carnegie library!

The reality of the job was even better than what I thought it would be—ten times better. The Director of the library gave me a free hand to do what I wanted to do, as long as I came up with a certain number of programs a month and got the newsletter done. I could work as many or as little hours a week as long as I got that done.

The best part of the job was my office. My very own office, with a huge desk. It was on a mezzanine, overlooking the main floor of the library, and the side that faced the library floor was all glass. The view I had was dark wood paneling, couches and chairs for reading, floor-to-ceiling windows, and a massive stone fireplace.

I was in heaven. And, because I did programs in the evening and had to close up when everyone left, I had a key to the library!

Sometimes, if I didn't get the newsletter done, I would continue to work on it after closing. I did that on a computer by the check-out desk on the main floor.

The library was hushed and dark (only the closing lights were on). I could almost imagine the characters of the books on the shelves coming out and dancing around while I worked. The library became my own magic kingdom then, as it and books had always been for me.

Because I always had a keen curiosity, I never ran out of program ideas. And Nyack was an artistic and diverse community with a rich source of artists, writers, film makers, and actors. You name it, we had it.

Carson McCullers had lived in Nyack and we had committed to doing a program honoring her. Because of that I had the pleasure of visiting McCullers' home (where she wrote *Ballad of a Sad Café* and *Member of the Wedding*) and of meeting Dr. Mary Mercer, her psychotherapist and later close friend for many years.

I visited Dr. Mercer's home high on a hill where she enjoyed a sweeping view of the Hudson River. I planned the program, with local actors reading portions of McCullers' writings. One of the actors who gave a reading was Ellen Burstyn, who lived in Upper Nyack.

When Karen Finley came to my office and said she wanted to do a program at the library, she explained in a soft-spoken voice that she was a performance artist and activist for women's rights. She had lost her National Endowment for the Arts grant based on a decency clause. She calmly stated that the government didn't have a right to decide what was decent and what wasn't.

I agreed to let her do a program because I didn't believe in censorship. I didn't realize how controversial and well-known she was. We usually had maybe an average of ten to twenty people come to a program. That night the line went up two flights of stairs and out the door. We had to estimate the number so it didn't exceed the fire code and had to turn some away.

Some members of the library board objected to it, but because of community support and praise, they only gave the Library Director advice to keep the programs less controversial.

We participated in a few programs developed by the County Library System; some we got grants for. One of those programs, Great Decisions, was popular. We would have discussions about foreign policy challenges facing Americans.

My favorite, though, was our yearly Book Discussion Series. Each series revolved around a specific topic, the county loaned us books that reflected the topic, and we hired scholars to lead the discussion.

There were other programs on a vast variety of topics: many authors, herbal remedies and acupuncture, demystifying dreams, opera, a batik workshop (presented by a local batik artist), flower arranging, getting organized, financial planning, Irish women poets, an Appalachian Trail slide show, a peace program by the Fellowship of Reconciliation, drawing, art lectures, among others.

For me, it was fun, educational, stimulating, and challenging. And I got to work in a magical place.

I often kidded Ernie, that if I ever ran away, he would know exactly where to look for me.[1]

1.  *Carnegie libraries were built with money provided by Scottish-American businessman Andrew Carnegie. There were 1,689 built in the United States between 1883 and 1929. Most of these libraries had impressive architecture. One of Carnegie's requirements was that the libraries have open shelving where patrons could browse and choose their own books, unlike the current system at the time where a patron had to request a particular book and someone would go and retrieve the requested item. Another requirement was that they have large, high windows to provide lighting.

# IT'S BEEN
# QUITE A RIDE

# Colorado Rocky Mountain High

My dream of a cross-country trip was born on a Saturday morning on Route 59 in Nanuet, New York. I was driving up Route 59 when I spotted a gold-colored van with a For Sale sign on it. I pulled over and got out. There was no price on it, so I didn't know if we could afford it. I peered inside through the window. Oh my gosh, I thought, as I looked. Shag carpet, tie-dyed curtains—and a peace sign on the back window! I couldn't wait to get home to tell Ernie about it.

When I got home, I urged him to come look at it with me. We went back, pulled over and got out. Ernie, as usual, was cautious and practical—looking it over carefully. I was jumping-up-and-down excited.

"Can we get it? Do you think we can afford it? Call. Call and ask."

I had fallen in love . . . instantly. I wanted it so badly; I couldn't stand the wait.

Wanderlust. Though I never got to put the actual word on the vehicle, in my heart that will always be its name.

After the actual purchase, Ernie began to outfit it to suit our needs—pale gray paneling, wiring for electrical, side windows that opened, a vent in the ceiling, seats for storage, a table be- tween the seats that lowered and created a bed for us, a cook- ing unit on the door complete with storage and a shelf for a portable stove.

The dream was blossoming.

We hoped to have it ready for a month-long trip after I graduated from RCC. We arranged to take the kids out of school a few weeks early (after all, what better education!). We told them, though, that they had to keep a journal.

Ernie diligently worked on his projects and arranged for the time off from work, while I sewed the curtains for the side windows and cushions for the seats/bed and started planning the actual trip. But there was a lot to do and the clock was ticking fast.

The day finally arrived. Saturday, June 7, 1975. Ernie was thirty-two, and I would turn thirty-two on the trip. Young Ernie would turn thirteen on the trip and Randy would be ten in October. We were all ready for a grand adventure.

We had planned to leave early—around 6:00 or 7:00 am—but, of course, that was overly optimistic.

After we packed everything up, including our tent and camping gear on a roof rack, off we went. Closer to 9:00 am.

The beginning of the trip, through **New York** and **New Jersey**, seemed snaillike. The whole rest of the country yawned before us. Finally, we reached **Pennsylvania** (after going through a thin slice of **West Virginia**), and what seemed like progress. The kids were excited by a series of tunnels that went through the Kittatinny Mountains and concerned when things on the rooftop began to come loose. We pulled over and Ernie secured what was loose and we continued on our way. A minor mishap quickly taken care of, and the rest of the first day lay before us.

In **Ohio**, we heard a radio station where the emcee sang the songs live. We stayed in a campground in Ohio, had dinner against a backdrop of a setting sun and the mooing of cows. This is farm country. The cool, brisk air felt so good and healthy.

At the end of the day, we had driven 500 miles and gone through five states!

**Day Two** held a little more interest. First stop, Indianapolis Motor Speedway and Museum in **Indiana**. We saw old racing cars, including one from 1912, which had the first rearview mirror ever used.

The afternoon brought us into **Illinois**. The sky was blue; the land was flat—pleasant, easy, somewhat monotonous. In some places, the land looked so rich it was almost black.

The most exciting part of the day was crossing the Mississippi River and seeing the Arch across the river in **Missouri** at sunset. The Gateway to The West set against the background of a magnificently streaked orange and blue sky with an old-fashioned steamboat in the foreground.

We finally found a campground late that night and fell into bed, looking up through the ceiling vent at a sky full of stars and waking to the sun rising outside my window.

I was disappointed we didn't have the time to go back to St. Louis and visit the Arch and the steamboat.

Day two of the trip held a few disappointments, but exhilarations too.

**Day Three**—the kids cleaned up the van, wrote in their journals and played games. The people were really friendly and helpful in Missouri, especially in the gas stations. Ernie had a little trouble with the car; an attendant helped him and wouldn't charge him.

We drove through Kansas City—Missouri and **Kansas**—and parts of the road that had been The Oregon Trail, where 200 years ago pioneers and settlers averaged twelve miles a day.
Hard to believe when we were doing about 250 a day.

The sky was so blue, the land so F L A T; you can see as far as the eye can see. God's country. You can understand why people out here are so religious.

A few bumper stickers: "Eat more possum" and "Goat ropers need love too."

**Day Four**—we followed the Santa Fe Trail to Dodge City, Kansas, and passed wheat fields, small oil wells, picturesque railroad towns, crowded feed yards where cattle are kept until they weigh about 1,000 pounds.

Dodge City was settled in 1872 when the Santa Fe RR built it. This made the hunting of buffalo accessible and attractive. A skilled hunter could earn $100 a day. At the time, it is estimated there were 24 million buffalo; by 1875, the herds were nearly exterminated.

The Dodge City Museum had memorabilia of the original doctor and dental offices, drug store, bank—but the most fun was the nickelodeon, which played a robust melody evocative of the era.

Back on the road, we spotted the Rockies. At first we thought they were clouds or a mirage.

We checked into The Garden of the Gods Campground. We had arrived: **Colorado.**

Maybe because we had played John Denver's tapes for much of the trip, often singing along, Colorado seemed to be emblematic of the whole trip.

**Day Five**—we got up early and headed for The Garden of the Gods Park with its dramatic views and its 300-foot sandstone rock formations that seemed to defy nature. The Balanced Rock, the great monolith. Huge towering formations, all housing hundreds of cooing pigeons, lent an eerie quality. All awesome spectacles, some dating back millions of years.

Then on to The Cave of the Winds, where gusts of wind traveled through it before the main entrance was boarded up. The gusts of wind had created a maze of underground formations—stalactites, stalagmites and ribbonlike forms, which had taken millions of years to create.

We took Gold Camp Road, where miners panned for gold in the mid-1800s, and went to a Ghost Town that had been abandoned years ago. The highlight here was a player piano.

We went to see Indian cliff dwellings, preserved from the Great Pueblo civilization, around 1100 A.D., and the museum there where we saw unearthed bones, pottery, arrowheads and baskets—and watched tribal dancers.

Finally, we camped at the foot of the mountains—rustic, wooded and beautiful. We hiked up to Monument Rock for spectacular views of the Rockies and the countryside. We had climbed the Rockies!

The sky was vast and spectacular; there were millions of stars and the moon was monstrous.

I was moved to sing the words to John Denver's "Rocky Mountain High," and I could almost feel like I was getting high on the vastness of the sky and the seemingly endless stars above and the lullaby playing in my head.

**Day Six**—We experienced a bit of local color—went to an authentic western rodeo. We saw bronco riding, calf roping and tying, bareback riding, barrel races. It was an experience that made me feel very patriotic.

Next stop: Pike's Peak.

Snow was blocking the road for the last three miles, so we only made it as far as Glen Cove—12,000 feet. The view from there was spectacular though. Now I understand what "purple mountain majesty, above the fruited plains" means.

Went into Manitou Springs, lovely little shops. A lot of well-preserved older cars. Everything so clean, friendly and well taken care of. Surrounded by nature.

The best of what America can be—no wonder they are so patriotic and religious.

It was incredible to be camping beneath the pines at the foot of the Rockies after such a day. My heart was full, listening to John Denver, over a bottle of wine, having fresh salad, a delicious dinner around a campfire, and roasting marshmallows later. I felt at home in this place I had never been before and was content under the shelter of the stars.

**Day Seven**—we headed north towards Denver. Mountains and sky seemed to go on forever—cloud formations like I've never seen before. Water was crystal clear and delicious. Beautiful rustic homes lined the hillsides. We passed Buffalo Bill's grave, old abandoned mining operations, snow-covered mountains looming in the distance, streams, sheer cliffs, red canyons.

Finally, **Utah**—awesome desolation. We stayed at a campground beneath red rock canyons. We were warned about huge, biting red ants, so decided not to cook that night, but instead ate at the log cabin restaurant at the campground.

**Day Eight**—We went to Arches National Park, where stone arches, windows, spires and pinnacles of various shapes dotted the landscape, evoking images of a variety of animals and people. We saw a lizard, cactus, desert flowers, beautiful and eerie driftwood, and Randy saw a rabbit.

When we stood by the Park Avenue passageway, it was so silent that I had the feeling that I was standing there between those massive columns at the dawn of man.

Standing beneath the North Window, an arch that frames the sky, I felt overwhelmed, almost as if I were an ant looking up the leg of a picnic table. That culmination of nature's majesty was spiritual.

The arches were formed from the action of water, wind, rain, frost and sun. The sand that formed them was deposited a mind-boggling 150 million years ago, which was then buried and hardened into rock. Those rocks were then uplifted, twisted and severely cracked several times. Erosion finally stripped away the overlying layers, and the original deposits were exposed to weathering. Water entered cracks and dissolved some of the cementing material. Cracks were widened into narrow canyons. Water, frost and wind enlarged some, smoothing their contours till large, graceful arches were the final creation.

Monument Valley Highway—no trees, no shade, no respite from the heat. Tumbleweed. No sign of human life anywhere you looked. Mammoth shapes hulking above us made me feel utterly insignificant. We saw a man walking along the highway and wondered where he could possibly be walking from or to. There was nothing in sight in either direction.

The living conditions on Navajo land were horrendous. Houses were mud cottages, wood shacks or red stone, and were mostly dusty and poorly kept. The atmosphere was barren and bleak. Old, abandoned cars, beer bottles and cans littered the area.

We finally reached a campground in Flagstaff, **Arizona**. No matter how hot it was during the day, the nights were still pretty cold.

**Day Nine**—We gained another hour, but we didn't realize it. So instead of getting up at 6am, we got up at 5am. We headed for the Grand Canyon and managed to get a site right in the National Park. The Canyon didn't look real, more like a painting. Seems to stretch on forever, with a little stream at the bottom that is actually the mighty Colorado River. The mules traveling down to the bottom of the canyon looked like little ants. Truly awesome in its magnificence and enormity.

The youngest rocks in the canyon are 200 million years old and contain remnants of sea life, proving that the area was at one time under water. There's also evidence of prehistoric life nearly 4,000 years ago.

We hiked along the rim and a short way down the canyon.

The sunset from Mojave Point highlighted the colors and the shadings of the canyon walls, which took on deeper and more magnificent hues as the sun set.

Each moment brought a completely different setting—a kaleidoscope of color and form.

We went to the campfire program—a talk about the wildlife living in the area.

**Day Ten**—It was sweltering when we got to Hoover Dam—114 degrees. This engineering marvel rescued a land continually plagued by too much water or too little, and provided hydro-electric power as well.

We took a tour where we learned that concrete for it was poured almost continually for nearly two years to construct the wall of the dam. The dam itself cost 49 million when it was completed in 1936. Lake Mead in the largest man-made reservoir in the country.

From there we went to Las Vegas, **Nevada**—an entirely different world. Bright lights and excess. We stayed in a motel with a pool and Randy and Ernie went swimming. Later we freshened up and drove down the Strip. The quantity, size and glitziness of the casinos was mind-boggling. We went to Circus Circus. There were circus acts, arcades and rides right in the lobby. I didn't know where to look first. The kids had a ball. It was Ernie's 13th Birthday. What a place to spend a birthday. We had dinner there and played some slots, enjoying complimentary drinks.

**Day Eleven**—We had a 66-cent breakfast at Holiday Showboat. It looked like a turn-of-the century steamboat surrounded by water. Ernie played roulette and let the kids watch from the balcony but lost pretty quickly. Had lunch at Circus Circus and watched one of the acts.

When we went outside, we experienced an incredible dust storm—half inch of dust in the van and you couldn't even see the sky. We let the kids go in the pool one more time. Buffet dinner for $5 each, Vive Paris show at the Aladdin. We squeezed in whatever we could on our last night in Vegas.

**Day Twelve**—We left at 5:30 to beat the heat crossing the desert —on only three hours sleep. Bye Vegas! **California**, here we come. The desert between Vegas and LA wasn't what I pictured— more vegetation, less sand, more hilly.

Beautiful shrubbery and palm trees line the highways in LA. We got a campsite and took a nap before heading to Disneyland. The best rides were Pirates of the Caribbean, the Haunted Mansion, bobsled ride down the Matterhorn, Monsanto's journey through a microscope. At Monsanto you could feel yourself shrinking to the size of a snowflake and then further into the microscopic world of a nucleus.

The 360-degree panoramic overview of America was quite a culmination to a trip across the country.

The fireworks display and the patriotic songs brought tears to my eyes. We took the monorail back to the campground (passing hundreds of oranges being loaded at Sunkist). What a day!

**Day Thirteen**—We went to Universal Studios after a leisurely breakfast of pancakes and blueberries at the campground. Tour took us to film locations for *The Sting, Butch Cassidy, Psycho* and *The Munsters.*

We also saw how they film the live action scenes against backgrounds of paintings and/or miniature mechanical devices. They picked me from the audience for a "screen test" and played the scenes back with the actors from *Emergency.*

We stopped for pizza on Ventura Highway. The drive out to the ocean through the canyons was spectacular. And the drive along the coast in the moonlight with the waves crashing along the beach and the lights on shore in the distance was pretty amazing too.

We couldn't find a campsite, so we decided to camp right along the coast highway in Malibu. We settled down for the night with a stunning view of the beach to wake up to in the morning.

**Day Fourteen**—What a view to wake up to.

On our way again! Stopped to see San Luis Obispo, and stayed in San Simeon so we could go to the Hearst Castle tomorrow. Got tickets for 8:20 am. The state park campground was full but some nice people let us share their site, which had a beautiful view of the Pacific.

We made burgers, baked potatoes and salad and had time to relax and savor, after a busy few days.

**Day Fifteen**—We took the bus up to San Simeon Castle, driving up through clouds and past zebras and livestock. The splendor and magnificence of the castle and grounds are some- thing that is hard to imagine. We toured the guest house first and thought it was the castle, it was so splendid. Graceful and delicate Carrara marble statues surrounded the pool area.

The Moorish details of the castle were accentuated by intricate custom-designed tiles. The rooms were designed specifically for Hearst's vast collection of art works and antiques, which determined the height and width of the rooms. The fireplaces were massive.

The indoor pool was inlaid with the most brilliant blue tiles interspersed with 24 carat gold.

During its heyday, the castle was host to Hollywood stars, politicians, millionaires, and famous. In its theater, Clark Gable watched the premiere of *Gone with the Wind*.

The coastline above San Simeon was spectacular—just as I imagined the Pacific Coast Highway to be: roads curving through the mountains, hanging precipitously above an ocean that was so blue it defied the imagination. There is no artist who could paint a prettier picture—the sky, the waves, pristine sandy beaches, huge rock formations against whose sides waves crashed. Perfection. Each turn brought a more dramatic vista.

After lunch along the highway, we stopped at Point Lobos State Park in Carmel that had interesting rock formations—a bunch of different rocks cemented together by sand that had hardened into unusual shapes.

We arrived at our friends' (Val and Ken Plam) place in Foster City. They were moving into a new home, which was beautiful, high on a hill, with a view of the Bay Area below. When you entered their home, you think you will be entering a living room or entryway, but it was an indoor garden with a moveable roof.

They made us dinner. We had a bottle of champagne and toasted their new home and seeing each other again, and they had a birthday cake for Ernie's 13th birthday.

We slept at their house in front of the fireplace.

**Day Sixteen**—After we had coffee, Ken drove us into San Francisco, through Chinatown, down Lombard St., to Fisherman's Wharf and the Cannery. We took a cable car ride and went to the Cable Car Museum. We went back to their house and had a swim in their pool while they moved a few more things. We were exhausted after a busy day.

That night we stayed at their old place.

**Day Seventeen**—We took a ride across the Golden Gate Bridge, which gave us a pretty view of San Francisco from the other side. We went to Muir Woods. The base of some of the redwoods there measured 13 feet in diameter and rose to the height of about 260 feet. Some of the stumps were weathered away and almost looked like pieces of modern sculptures.

We stopped in Sausalito where we went into a few shops and saw a strange conglomeration of houseboats—beautiful modern ones, one an old steamboat, some with stained-glass windows, weird shapes, in fact, every shape and size.

We went back to Fisherman's Wharf. The kids went to a magic show while we did a little shopping. Then we went to Ghirardelli Square and all the little shops there. We just made it back to Val's in time for dinner. They really made us feel at home, and it was a nice break after camping for the past two weeks.

**Day Eighteen**—We stopped by to say good-bye to Valerie, so we got a late start. Stopped for lunch in Auburn, the site of the gold discovery that started the Gold Rush. We went to the museum there. Around Lake Tahoe, we started seeing signs saying ice and snow ahead. We really didn't believe it, but sure enough snow began to appear on the hillsides as we started to climb, and before long we found ourselves in a winter wonderland. Camped in Winnemucca.

We went right to sleep after dinner. Was it cold!

**Day Nineteen**—We got a late start, but we finally crossed the border into Utah. We passed the Bonneville Salt Flats, which is actually the residue of a prehistoric lake of which the Great Salt Lake is just a small part. The land-speed record of 622mph was set here in 1970. We stopped to put our feet into the Great Salt Lake. The sand was sooo smooth.

Along the Salt Flats as we were approaching Salt Lake City, we saw mirages—heavenly images. Reflections of the mountains in the water. In Salt Lake City itself the Mormon Temple rose majestically above the rest of the city, whose other buildings were relatively low. It had been built in the 1800s; I tried to imagine what it must have looked like at that time, towering over a small pioneering town.

For me, celebrating my birthday today, one of its best features was that it was across the street from a Baskin and Robbins, where I got a special treat—three scoops! What a birthday!!!

**Day Twenty**—The drive between Brigham City and the Idaho border was lovely—streams, pine forests, canyons. The Bear River, on the Utah/Idaho border, was stunning—its brilliant color changed from blue to blue-green to green, as the road curved this way and that.

We stopped for lunch and walked the trails a bit around Geneva (the southeast corner of **Idaho**), before crossing into **Wyoming**. We rode along the Snake River and saw people riding the rapids—looked exciting. We went into a few of the shops in Jackson and discovered the mythical creature, the jackalope—a rabbit with antelope horns. We made arrangements for a White Water Rafting trip for tomorrow morning. We settled in at the campsite, excited about the adventure tomorrow.

**Day Twenty-one**—Rafting down the Snake River was quite the adventure. If the wave didn't break when you rode it, it was such a soft float over it; if it broke, it was so thrilling you could feel it in the pit of your stomach. But it was freezing when the water washed over the side.

And did we get wet! When we got back to the campsite, I made pancakes before we drove up through the Tetons to Yellowstone. The sky was blue, clear and beautiful as the road curved along the river, evergreens in the foreground, the jagged, barren stone as a backdrop, and the snow-covered peaks rising above us.

We entered Yellowstone and its beauty took my breath away. I had always heard a lot about Old Faithful, but not much about the rest of the park. In reality, Old Faithful is just a small, almost insignificant, part of this fascinating, compelling National Park. Its eerie beauty brought me back to the days when the earth was still being formed. Boiling water erupts beneath its surface creating an array of colors and weird phenomena. Pink bubbling volcanic-like pools, brilliant orange waterfalls cascading down ice-like rock cliffs, steam gushing from pools and mountainsides. Each location presented an entirely new creation of nature brought about by volcanic lava one and a half miles below the surface of this area, which was once the crater of one of the largest volcanoes on earth. There were magnificent waterfalls and snow-capped mountains set against a large, impressive lake.

Finally, we were able to secure a campsite, ate dinner and drove to see Old Faithful. On the way back in the dark, it started to snow.

Day Twenty-two—Before we left Yellowstone, we went to see the Upper Falls, Lovers' Falls, Obsidian Cliff, and the spectacular Mammoth Hot Springs. We stopped to have lunch along the Yellowstone River, just across the **Montana** border. Now I understand why they call this Big Sky Country. We stopped early in Billings and got a campsite right alongside the river underneath some huge trees, giving us some time to relax and barbeque before going to bed. Lovely.

Day Twenty-three—We got an early start. We stopped at Custer National Battlefield. Interesting to be in the area where these historical events took place. The surrounding hillsides are relatively untouched by time, so it is easy to picture the Indians camped along the river, Custer and his men riding up and catching a glimpse of their inevitable downfall—thousands of Indians camped below whose size Custer had fatally underestimated. After leaving the battlefield we saw some Indians actually living in a tepee.

We entered **South Dakota** and the Black Hills, or should I say red, since the hillsides were mostly reddish clay with pine trees. We drove to where the Lakota Indians commissioned a Polish-American sculptor to create a monument of Chief Crazy Horse. He has been working on the project for 28 years. He envisioned it finished in seven or eight years. He had a dream of an Indian Center, university and airport, and he dedicated his life to fulfilling it. Then his sons continued the project.

Mt. Rushmore seemed dwarfed after seeing the Crazy Horse undertaking. Of particular interest were the eyes of the presidents, which must be viewed through binoculars to fully appreciate of their captivating effect.

We took Needles Parkway back to the campsite—hairpin turns that could make your hair stand up, tunnels carved out of the rock that you could barely squeeze through. The steep climbs, the increasing darkness and an impending storm made it even hairier.

Monstrous, menacing clouds moved in, dwarfing the existing clouds. There were holes in the clouds where a brilliant blue sky showed through. Lightning lit up the whole sky as the storm raged. When we got back to the campground, we breathed a sigh of relief. There it was, calm and beautiful with a clear sky above and a million stars, but the storm still raged on the horizon.

**Day Twenty-four**—We headed for the Badlands, after an early morning start. Along the highway we kept seeing signs for Wall Drugs (Wall Drugs 200 miles, Wall Drugs 175 miles, etc., etc., etc.). Finally, we got to the small town of Wall and the exit for, you guessed it, Wall Drugs. Our curiosity got the better of us and we exited.

We had breakfast—49 cents for eggs and 69 cents for French toast and 5 cents for coffee. It's quite a national phenomenon! Written up in Playboy and the Wall St. Journal, it attracts 10,000 people a day and does $1 million dollars of business a year. They have signs advertising its wares as far off as Paris, Amsterdam and Vietnam. It's a maze of little shops—indoors and out—and is really quite something.

We finally got to the Badlands, which were similar to Utah with more shades of color and more greenery.

The kids, by this time, were sick of writing in their journals and looking at the sights. The hues and striations of color were brilliant, and I wanted them to see them, so I told them, "You'll look out the window and like it!" Well, they did, but I don't think they liked it.

The heat was oppressive. We finally found a park with shade and had lunch. We camped on Lake Mitchell and took a dip in the lake to cool off. Then we went to see the Corn Palace. This Moorish-style building is decorated each year with scenes created by people in the area with three colors of corn—yellow, golden and brown.

The rest of Mitchell was like going back to the 50s in a time machine. Main St. USA, where kids (pony-tail types in Bermuda shorts and greasers) cruised in their souped-up cars (some 40s and 50s models).

**Day Twenty-five**—We drove through **Minnesota**, which was boring from one end of the state to the other.

It was early evening when we crossed the Mississippi River into **Wisconsin** and realized that our cross-country trip was coming close to an end.

My journal ends there. I remember going through Wisconsin Dells and then Chicago. I think after that we were just in a rush to get home.

Looking at the route we took and where certain things were located on the map, I may have gotten a few things muddled up the last few days and maybe even lost a day or perhaps two. The 25th day would have been July 1, a Tuesday. Ernie went back to work on Monday, July 7, and I don't remember being home for four days before he had to go back to work.

I recall two incidents that I did not record in my journal. They both involved bears. At one of the campgrounds, the boys wanted to sleep outside in their small pup tent. We let them, but in the middle of the night I heard noises and got scared and made Ernie go out and get them.

At one of the National Parks, there was a warning against camping in tents. We didn't, but when we woke in the morning our campground neighbor asked us if we had heard the bear that was looking in our van window during the night.

That image scared the heck out of me.

I think if I had to choose, I would say that Utah and Wyoming were the two states that surprised me the most with their beauty. In any case, it was a grand adventure—twenty states and almost 8,000 miles—and a wonderful education for the kids about our country, how incredibly diverse and stunning it is.

We found out that we had been quite lucky in our journey. We had missed an earthquake in Yellowstone, a hailstorm in Billings, and a snowstorm in the Rockies. We did manage to hit record cold in the Rockies (30 degrees), where we had to purchase a heater for the van, and record heat at Hoover Dam (116 degrees; it was only 114 degrees when we were there), but we managed to do okay overall.

My dream of a cross-country journey was complete and there were many more camping adventures ahead for us and our trusty van, Wanderlust.

# Where Your Story Begins

Home may be where your story began, but that was light years ago. It was just the opening sentence of a book yet to be written. Yet, at times, I've allowed it to weave its way into the current chapter—an errant sentence. The reader might say, "What?Where did that come from?" I forgot it was in chapter one and is redundant, has little place in chapter 18, or 40, or 62. It's just background information so you understand the character or the current story.

"Where are you now, woman?" seems to call me to task. I have at times written the end already, impatient to see how it turns out, rather than letting the chapters unfold, character driven, not plot driven, not some story board that has to end in a certain way.

"Where are you, woman?" The brain, the heart, the vagina, the soul? Must we choose? I am all these—a complicated package, that is more than the sum of its parts.

Home may have been where my story started, but the story has taken me further than I ever imagined. I never imagined that I would go to Europe, much less to have traveled to Holland, Ireland, Northern Ireland, Scotland, France, Italy, Austria, Switzerland, Spain, and England; that we would drive cross-country, and visit 47 of the 50 states; that we'd own a motorcycle and an airplane; that we'd ever live anywhere other than New York; and that we'd have such a large, wonderful family.

It's been quite a ride.

# Boone's Farm

Can you imagine we actually drank that stuff?
Thought we were cool.
In our '69 van
with its tie-dye curtains,
peace sign on the back window.


Wheels that gave us freedom,
took us cross-country,
through the endless plains of mid-America,
to the foot of the Rockies–
and beyond.


Boone's Farm wine accompanied us,
along with John Denver
singing "Rocky Mountain High"
around the campfire.


We were high–
high on life,
high on dreams and innocence.
High on the energy of hope.
In the '60s.

Many years and miles later,
cleaning out the van to sell,
we found a bottle
tucked under the seat.


Forgotten,
like that lost summer
of our youth.


Boone's Farm.
We looked at each other
And smiled

# Heavenly Highway

According to Charles Kuralt, the Beartooth Highway is "the most scenic highway in America." After flying into Billings, Montana, and staying overnight in Red Lodge, Ernie and I woke early with anticipation. Traveling southwest on Route 212, we started our ascent. I was psyched.

Rather than the thrill of spectacular scenery, however, everything was shrouded in a dense fog, covering all but the road directly ahead of us. Each moment brought with it intense disappointment, as I imagined all that I was missing. But, because we had plans and reservations for the trip ahead, we had no choice but to continue on.

I felt that, after traveling 2,000 miles to explore this American treasure, all that I was going to remember was driving through this soup. I wanted to yell, "No. Go back. I want to start over."

We drove along the winding road, snaking farther and farther into the heavens, the fog getting denser and denser. With each mile my tension and disappointment increased.

All of a sudden, out of the mist, rising up above us, like a monolithic monster out of a Scottish lake, stood a craggy mountain. We had risen above the clouds and for a while it was like driving on a soft pillow. A heavenly highway.

The clouds soon dissipated to display majestic vistas everywhere you looked. They were spectacular. All the more so, for their sudden appearance. I let out a breath.

For the next fifty or so miles, at times traveling along the edge of nothing, feeling like a mountain goat, the road snaked up the mountainside in a series of tight switchbacks up to the 10,000-foot summit, then back down again through Montana and Wyoming. Each bend unfolding a different landscape, one more splendid than the next.

Along the way we saw a sharp-peaked stone—the bear's tooth—that rose out of the granite mountains looking as if it were plucked from the top of one of the pyramids of Egypt.

Another scene showed the curving road spiraling out before us. Another a lake, placid and bucolic, an oasis amidst the rugged glacially carved mountains. Peaks and valleys. Around a sharp bend, a sudden precipitous drop. An otherworldly landscape waited around the next bend. Mist still caressed parts of the mountain, draping it like a mystical veil.

Mr. Kuralt did not exaggerate

# Flying High

Ernie and I flew up to Block Island for the day in our four-seater airplane. We've had the plane for about twenty years. The plane is Ernie's mistress, but I don't mind the time he spends with her. It's an older model Cessna 172, which has been meticulously cared for and has a beautiful paint job, so we often get compliments when we fly somewhere.

I hadn't been flying with Ernie in a while, but I always love flying to Block Island. My motto is: I don't like flying for the sake of flying, but fly me somewhere for lunch and I'll go.

While Ernie was doing his pre-flight checklist, I put my headphones on and buckled myself in. I get a little apprehensive when I haven't been up flying in a while, especially when the winds buffet the plane around a bit. Ernie is a careful pilot with over forty-five years' experience, so I know I am in good hands. So off we went.

After we took off, I got so caught up in the views from the air that I forgot to be nervous.

Channels, lakes, and bays were illuminated when the sun moved over them. Small ponds became glittering diamonds when the sun shimmered across their surfaces. Boaters created trails like writhing snakes, while others cut straight arrows in the water, their destinations clear. One spit of land on the South Fork reached out like a pointy finger at the North Fork, accusatory and brash. A patchwork quilt of colorful towels and umbrellas dotted the beach.

We flew high but close to land whenever we could, a precaution

Ernie always takes when we fly over an expanse of water, just in case something happens. It was only when we were over open water that a bit of my apprehension returned, but Ernie landed safely and easily. We headed to town for lunch. It's about a mile away so we usually walk there since it's mostly downhill. We do, however, take a taxi back.

I had a lunch of succulent medium-rare tuna, coleslaw with wasabi and a mimosa at the Harbor Grill, overlooking the water.

We left The Block and headed home. It looked like a hop, skip and a jump to the tip of Montauk, but it was fifteen minutes before we passed over it. It always amazes me to see how much undeveloped land there is out near Montauk, miles and miles of untouched shoreline and forest.

Heading back over Napeague and Peconic bays, the water was darker, the boats more numerous and all heading for shore. They looked like lightning bugs lighting up the night sky.

Again, I saw acres of protected land between Hampton Bays and Westhampton. I looked on Ernie's navigation map and saw that they were Hubbard County Park and Sears Bellows County Park. How great it is that others thought to protect all this land for us to enjoy.

Finally, I saw the runway of Gabreski Airport and I started to breathe easier as I came closer to having two feet on the ground again and another nice adventure to file in my memory bank.

Perfect day, perfect weather. These gems don't come along all the time, and when they do you must capture and savor them!

# 29 Years—
# 20,000 Miles

September, 1989—"Who goes to a wedding and buys a motorcycle?" Ernie asks at the back of a small Harley dealer in upstate New York. We were on our way to a wedding near Buffalo.

"Yeah, but isn't it beautiful! I never saw a bike that color."

"How would we get it home? It's kind of pricey."

For me it was love at first sight. Ernie, more deliberate and practical, needed more time.

"It's the prettiest bike I've ever seen." And it was—a rust-colored Harley with a brown leather seat and custom white fiberglass saddlebags and luggage rack with pin-striping. A beauty, indeed.

We had stopped for a bite to eat in the tiny one-horse town of Varysburg. After lunch we thought we'd stretch our legs a bit before we continued our drive.

There was a Harley Davidson dealer up the block and not much else. We decided to take a look. We owned a smaller motorcycle—a Yamaha 650. We weren't really in the market for a new bike, but it's always fun to look at other motorcycles, especially for Ernie.

Me, I had hoped for an antique shop or two.

It was a small dealership, and because it was at the V-shaped intersection of Routes 98 and 20A, the front of the place was narrow and it widened at the back.

Ernie lingered at the front of the store, chatting with the owner.

I ventured to the back of the shop where they had some used bikes, and there it was: OUR Harley.

"Ernie, come here. Look at this."

Our Yamaha had taken us on short rides near our house, but it was much smaller and less powerful than a Harley, and it certainly wasn't as comfortable as this bike. I began to envision places this machine could take us. I had always imagined that in a different time and place, I would have been an explorer. I loved going to new places, discovering small towns and back roads—taking the scenic route through life.

We had married young—just out of high school—and had two sons by the time we were twenty-two. Our sons were twenty-seven and twenty-four and pretty much on their own. We had built our life around family, but now it was our time. I was ready to make up for missed years of being young and free. The open road and a Harley seemed a good place to start.

On our way home after the wedding, I said to Ernie, "I think that Harley has your name on it."

Back home, I just couldn't get that Harley out of my mind. Things I've heard about Harleys began to play through my head at odd times during the day: Live to Ride, Ride to Live; The Road Starts Here, It Never Ends. I wanted it to never end: our love story, our sharing things we enjoyed, having fun together.

Live free and ride a Harley.

Ernie, too, was haunted by thoughts of the bike.

He did some research. He called the dealer and asked a number of questions about it. A deal was struck. Now, how would we get the bike home?

"Well, I could drive you up there, drive the car back, and you could ride the bike," I said.

"I don't have plates or insurance. Besides, I don't want my first ride to be a five-hour trip. I want to get used to it first."

So, he arranged to take a good-sized van home from work the following Friday. His co-workers could take the seats out in order to fit the motorcycle in the van. He called the dealer and told him he would come on Saturday to pick up the bike.

As the week wore on, we began to hear about the threat of a hurricane. Ernie decided to go anyway. He left after work on Friday, hoping to beat the storm. He brought his sleeping bag so he could stop overnight when he got tired without the bother of having to look for a motel.

As I waited at home, I looked out the window to see the rain coming down and the wind whipping the big old trees in the front of the house. These were the days before cell phones, so I had no idea what was happening with Ernie. I was glued to the TV and saw the storm continue to worsen. Hurricane Hugo made landfall near Charleston, South Carolina, around midnight on September 22, 1989, as a Category 4 hurricane, with winds up to 140 mph; I was still awake wondering where he was and if he was okay.

When I woke the next morning, the storm had passed, but I still worried about how Ernie was. Finally, the phone rang. I ran to get it, "Ernie?"

"Yeah."

"Are you okay? Did you get it?"

"Yeah. Yeah. I'll tell you all about it when I get home. I should be there in about two or three hours."

"Okay, Hon. Be careful."

To keep myself busy till he got home, I started to make some chicken cutlets. The kids came home and were hungry, so that kept me busy. It was getting dark, but still no sign of him. I was hoping Ernie would get home before the kids went out for the evening. Finally, I saw the headlights turn into our driveway.

He was home.

I wanted to hear everything. Immediately. But he was hungry and tired. Ugh. I hate waiting. I knew the routine, he would go to the bathroom, wash up, have something to eat. But no, he asked the kids to help him put the motorcycle in the garage. They went out and surveyed the situation. Ernie turned the van around, facing the garage, and got two long planks of wood to create a ramp. He unhooked the tie downs anchoring the bike, and slowly and carefully led the bike down the ramp. I stood on the side, feeling like I should be doing something. All of a sudden, the bike veered off the ramp and the three of them struggled to right the heavy machine. I darted ahead to help. For just a moment before they got it back on track, I felt the weight. It startled me, the heft of it.

I was so caught up in the effort to unload the bike that I hardly looked at it much until they had it off the ramp.

Wow. Wow!

Later, Ernie and I sat at the table in the kitchen. There was a bottle of wine someone had given us a while back that we were saving for a special occasion. He uncorked it and poured; we clinked glasses. "To us and the road ahead," I said.

While eating the chicken cutlets, he told me about his adventure. "Lynn, you wouldn't believe how the wind was rocking the van. There was a while there when I thought the van would blow over, it was shaking so hard. I was so tired, though, that I fell asleep pretty quick. When I woke up in the morning, it was totally calm."

"What time did you get up?"

"It was pretty early. Too early to go to the Harley place, so I went for breakfast in that little place where we ate lunch."

"So, what happened when you went over to the dealer? Did the bike look as good as we remembered?"

"Yeah, but when I looked it over, I saw that the rear tire was pretty worn. I tried to get him to throw in a new one. He said he would replace it and give me a break on the price. I said okay, but I wasn't happy. Then I took it for a test drive. It handles pretty nice."

"Do you want another glass of wine?"

"No, I just want to sleep in my own bed."

"Well, tell me more before you do."

"We had trouble getting the bike in the van. We realized after the first try that it wasn't going to fit with the windshield on. So, we had to back it out, remove the windshield and try again. Even then it barely fit. We strapped it down real good."

"You look tired."

"It was a long day. I'm gonna take a shower and head to bed. See you in the morning, Hon."

"Good night, Babe."

Ernie took the bike out a few times by himself.

While he was at work, once in a while I would go into the garage and look it, anticipating our first ride together.

Finally, the day came and Ernie wheeled the bike out of the garage and onto the driveway.

The air was crisp with fall. I put my helmet on and my leather gloves, then tried to get on the bike. The Yamaha was smaller and easy to get on. The Harley was so big I had to swing my leg up and around and hop on. Definitely different. Off we went.

The roar of the engine—the distinctive sound of a Harley—broke the stillness of the afternoon.

One of our favorite rides with the Yamaha was Seven Lakes Drive, just south of Bear Mountain. Its endlessly winding roads are a delight on a motorcycle. The passenger has to lean into a turn when the road curves. I always loved this on the Yamaha; I would lean left and right, in rhythm with Ernie, the bike and the road.

The Harley was different, it didn't lean as easily and it felt stiffer, almost like it would fall over if I leaned in. It took a while to get the hang of it. As we turned a corner, the raw red and orange of one tree amidst others clad in green popped out at me, and I felt my body begin to relax. It was a much smoother ride than the Yamaha, better for longer excursions.

Those early years, with both kids grown and on their own, we rode free, the wind in our faces. Without the intrusion of car doors and windows, there was no separation between us and the world. Every tree and building was sharply delineated against the blue sky.

We moved in and out of the shade of trees—cool, warm, cool,

warm. Everything had an added intensity. The smells, temperature changes, sounds were heightened.

All of a sudden, roads I had been down numerous times before morphed into unknown territory. Details, unnoticed before, emerged like props on a stage set.

There are few moments in adulthood where we can recapture the sense of freedom and joy we had as children—the joy I felt rolling down a hill at the Resey or riding my bicycle down Kimball Avenue or my sleigh down Coutant hill. Moments of exhilaration I was able to recapture on the back of the motorcycle. Older now, the years slipped away and we were young again, the wind whipping past, the road winding ahead of us.

When riding, distractions and problems faded away and I was in the zone, a moving meditation. The world and its problems disappeared; it was a true escape. On the bike, I allowed the intensity, the exhilaration of the experience inhabit the moment.

At first, we rode fairly close to home—Bear Mountain, Cold Spring, West Point, Storm King. We would stop for lunch, explore antique shops and quaint little towns, go for ice cream. Always an adventure. Then we traveled farther afield, going to Woodstock and Big Indian and byways throughout Connecticut, and into the Berkshires, once venturing up to Laconia, New Hampshire, and once to Lake George.

We went to a few motorcycle events, ones where there were bikes parked as far as the eye could see, hundreds. There were men and women in leathers, with tattoos and chains, all ages. Others looked like they were Monday-to-Friday executives, living out a parallel life on the weekends. Most were very nice, but some looked positively scary.

I remember getting a kick out of one tough-looking guy, talking to his friends, saying he had to head home. He had promised to iron his wife's dress for a wedding.

One very memorable event we went to was Rolling Thunder in New York City. It had started in 1988 as a demonstration to show support for Vietnam Veterans.

The year we did it, we began the run in Rockland County, and were joined along the way by other groups of riders. Riding through some narrow streets, our thunder set off numerous car alarms. We gained in numbers till we converged from north, south, east and west in Liberty Park. With our toll paid ahead of time, we continued with a police escort through the Holland Tunnel and down the West Side Highway, which were closed to other vehicular traffic. It is hard to describe the cacophony of hundreds of motorcycles reverberating off the sides of the tunnel. The destination was Battery Park for a Vietnam Veterans memorial service.

There are a handful of times when my heart has swelled with patriotism. This was one of them.

In 1976, it was the 100th birthday of the Statue of Liberty. Ernie and I had been watching TV coverage of the event, which was supposed to include a spectacular fireworks display by Grucci. Ernie turned to me and said, "This is crazy, people are coming from all over the United States to see this and we're here watching it on TV. It's a beautiful evening, let's go."

"You're crazy! You know what the traffic is going to be like?"

"We'll take the motorcycle and go down along the Hudson and see how close we can get."

Well, we did. We wended our way down, squeezing between and around cars like all those other crazy motorcyclists do, until we found ourselves not far from Liberty Park, where you have a view across the Hudson to the Statue of Liberty. As we got closer Ernie didn't want to drive much farther because the traffic was getting heavy and he was afraid the bike might not be too safe in the park itself. He found a place to park, and we joined the rest of those who were walking.

As the night sky lit up against the backdrop of Lady Liberty with her arm raised high, we were dazzled by the breathtaking display with the Manhattan skyline in the background. No other fireworks could ever live up to those we saw that night in Liberty Park.

In 1995, life took us to Rochester Hills, Michigan. The Harley came along with us. The roads there were straighter and level. Some of our favorite rides were Lexington, a charming little harbor village right on the shore of Lake Huron; Port Huron and across the Blue Water Bridge, so named for the tropical color of the waters of Lake Huron, and into Canada and along the shoreline; taking a small ferry from Marine City across the St. Clair River to Canada and tooling around.

The Harley came with us when we moved back to New York in 2006. There we enjoyed a few short rides on the East End of Long Island—to Westhampton, Montauk and Sag Harbor. But times had changed and so had we. Drivers were crazier. Traffic was heavier, especially during tourist season. And we were older. We finally faced reality and sold the bike in 2018.

We rode that bike with the wind at our backs for 29 years and 20,000 miles—far and wide. We rode free. It was love at first sight, and parting was sweet sorrow. But it was time.

# Story of a Marriage

How does one tell the story of a marriage? How do I sum up the days and nights, the ups and downs, of sixty years together? How do I convey the love, the passion, the depths, the complexities? How do I do that without cliches?

Not easily.

Do I say he breathes in, I breathe out? Do I say he understands me and still loves me? Do I say that being together is one of my greatest pleasures, but that being apart enriches both of us? Do I say that our life together is more than I ever dreamed it would be? Do I say that we have inside jokes based on a lifetime together that nobody would get but us, that there are memories I couldn't share with anyone else if something ever happened to him? Do I say that we have traveled so many places, shared so many of those memories, that it seems hard to believe that it's only been one lifetime? Do I say that we look at our family–our two sons, our daughters-in-law, our seven grandchildren–and swell with pride and joy in the lives they are creating? Do I say that his touch still makes me tingle? Do I say that in his arms I am home?

Or do I just say that it has been a lifelong love affair?

# AGING ...
# SOMETIMES WITH GRACE

# Wise Woman

I try to envision an older, wiser self. I feel like I am growing into that persona. I have an image of a little girl in dress-up clothes—all pink and gauzy, drooping off the shoulder, heels wobbling trying to find a foothold. I am that little girl with wistful eyes learning to be my wiser self—seeking the balance, twirling in delight as I look in the mirror and get a glimpse of her now and then.

Other days, I close the trunk and forget the garments hidden there for me to rummage through, but it is always there if I take the time.

I dream of the day when this wise woman can be my daily companion—my spiritual guide—and we can walk hand-in-hand and side-by-side on steady feet and a sure path.

# Off the Beaten Path

Women who step off the beaten path—the path dictated for them by previous generations, by when and where they were born, by expectations of their families—are brave. My grandmother was such a woman, destined for the poverty of Glasgow slums, a woman destined to bear children early and often, a woman blessed instead with a plain face, a stout spirit and an adventurous heart. I say blessed with a plain face, because she was not the most marriageable, stayed unmarried after what was considered marriageable age, scandalized the family by becoming a nurse at a time when it was unseemly for a woman to do so. Then, in another bold move, she set off for America with hardly a backward glance.

She had to create a path where none had gone before, through thorny bushes and rocky terrain.

She did have that husband and the expected family—five girls and one boy—but it turned out that it wasn't the easiest road she could have taken, offering her little solace, but many challenges and heartbreak.

Her second oldest daughter, my mother, too, went off the beaten path a bit. Ambitious, she worked in a factory during wartime like many women, but she refused to settle for an apron and the kitchen as she was expected to do when the men returned. Instead, she forged a career and got involved in politics, getting elected as councilwoman from a district in Yonkers.

Always good with figures, she went to night school to learn accounting and when the building burnt down and she was out of a job, she took advantage of the opportunity to apply for a job as an accountant, but soon found out she couldn't get a job as an accountant without experience. With a little hutzpah and a lot of luck, she told one employer she had worked as an accountant at the place that had burned down, and because all their records burned in the fire, they were unable to verify that. They hired her anyway. That was the start of her career as an accountant, which ended when she retired from Pepsi Cola Headquarters in Purchase, New York.

I, too, have forged a different path. I was determined that I would break the chain of alcoholism and craziness that prevailed in my family. I wanted a different kind of life for any children that I had. Of my fifteen or so cousins, only a few have "escaped" that family pattern. I am proud to say I am one of them.

I am my grandmother's granddaughter: I have stepped off the beaten path

# Seasons

Fall creeps up on you just when summer seems at its fullest, when you are bursting with your strongest sense of yourself—beyond that spring when you had to force out your buds and the budding was so hard and you were always watching for dangers: March winds shaking your branches, too much watering or too little, wild life threatening your flowers.

Summer comes and days are long; everything is in bloom under azure skies. What happened to the summers of my youth that stretched languorously before me? Days so long you forget and sleep the days away. You are soothed into complacency, listening to the Sirens' song of summer, lulled into thinking they would go on forever.

And then, without warning, you awaken and the day is cold. Leaves are changing and you hadn't noticed. They've lost that germinating greenness. They try to cling to the trees, but it is inevitable.

I've always had trouble letting go, yet life is a process of letting go. As we age, the losses pile up: friends and family fall away. Hair thins and grays, ears no longer hear well, legs and back tire and hurt, sleep eludes, sex drive wanes.

How does one grow lovely growing old?

The tree or shrub with useless limbs, grows sturdier with their loss. Stronger. Likewise, letting go of old sorrows and problems should make us freer, closer to inner serenity.

I walk the beach and observe the crash of angry waves and the gentle wash of others. The tides rhythmic, ebbing and flowing, leaving shells and sea glass in their wake. That's how I want the rest of my life to be: peaceful and rhythmic—in the flow.

But I am still frantic with choices. I have the hungry eyes of the young girl at the start of life's path. How, then, do I proceed in this diminishing world of aging?

Yes, even if I think I will live to be 100, having hit 75, I can't deny that I am in the winter of my life.

I strive for the brass ring, reaching with yoga stretches, writing for wisdom and insight, shedding what doesn't work. Saying no to wasted time, and yes to joy.

Is it in the surrendering to the moment, by giving up the striving, that true contentment exists?

# The Days Fly By

We are all born to a world of change,
Though we may never know why.
We grow and learn, despair, rejoice,
Wonder, and laugh and cry.
. . . And the days fly by.
And some look back with little more
Than regret and a wistful sigh,
Or worry their way toward the future,
Or do their best to deny that the days fly by.
Each moment in time is a gift
That comes and goes in the blink of an eye.
We question, as always, the meaning of life,
And "to live" is the only reply.
So I celebrate you in the here and now.
May you live as well as life will allow,
And may your spirits be ever high,
So they, too, fly
. . . As the days fly by.
   —*Anonymous*

# Valedictory Speech—Years in the Making

I've thought many times of the Valedictory speech I was asked to give when I was in my 20s. I've thought of what I would have said. It has changed numerous times over the years. Now I'll tell you what that twenty something wouldn't have said that this eighty-year-old would.

- The practice of gratitude has enhanced my life. By enumerating the things that make me happy during a day—often very simple things like a beautiful sunset, a text from a grandchild, a call from one of my sons or a friend, an especially good meal, enjoying some time by the ocean or with my Sweetie—made me take notice of them more, increased my happiness and made me more grateful. You are what you focus on.
- If you have a choice between being right or being happy, choose happy. You don't always have to prove a point or win every argument.
- I've found that one of the most important traits to have is resilience, the ability to recover quickly from difficulties. Trees that bend in the wind, don't break. We can't always control what happens to us, but we can change our response to it. Life is change. The quicker you move on, the happier you'll be.

- Let it go. Time is our most valuable gift; it is life itself. I have wasted valuable time throughout my life— thinking, worrying, cluttering my mind. The result of which is that you give a portion of your life away— minutes, hours, days—that you can never get back. Never ruin a good day by thinking about a bad yesterday or about something that might happen in the future. Be in the moment.
- Carpe Diem. Seize the day. Don't wait for the perfect time or situation, or for retirement. Say the things you want to say to the people you want to say them. Try something you've always wanted to try. Travel while you can. It is the best education. When you look back on your life, you won't say I should have worked more. You will regret not spending time with those you love, doing the things you enjoy, seeing some of the world and its delights.
- Love, friends, and family make life worth living.
- Although I haven't always been successful, I've created a mantra as a reminder of how best to live my life—with GRACE:
Gratitude
Resilience
Acceptance
Contentment
Enthusiasm
- Give yourself time alone to think about your life, how you're spending your time, your priorities. We don't, unfortunately, often get to do this while we are in the thick of things—forging a marriage, building a career, raising a family. There were many times when if I had done that it would have been helpful. So, take a step back every once in a while in your busy lives and PONDER.
- And, finally, never give up on yourself. We are all works

in progress...till the end. Each day is an opportunity to live better...wiser.

# The Legacy

November 11, 1970, Veteran's Day. My father had the day off. Despite the fact that he had emphysema and cirrhosis of the liver, he spent a good part of the day at the dinette table at 220 Kimball Avenue smoking and drinking beer. By the end of that day, he was dead.

I still have a hard time believing that he was only 59. The last time I saw him he had looked closer to 80—gray-haired, ill-kempt and slouching.

The tears I shed at his wake surprised me. I didn't cry so much for his loss, but for the sadness of his life. It appeared to me that there were few who mourned him. Had his life mattered? Or was it pointless?

When I found out that he had left me $5000 (about $40,000 today), I was determined that this legacy of his would mean something. It had to.

We had never owned new car, even though Ernie worked for GM and could get a discount. We took vacations, but usually on a budget. We rarely ate out at a restaurant. We lived very frugally.

Even though it would be nice to splurge, Ernie agreed that it was found money and I should use it to make a difference.

I didn't get the money until the estate was settled, perhaps a year or so later. At first, I thought we should buy a piece of property in New City that we could build on later. New City was an up-and-coming community, and it seemed to me that it would be a good investment. I started looking around at property. When we discussed it, I realized that he had little interest in building a house. He had spent a few years as a teenager helping his dad build theirs. He saw the headaches involved in building, and he wanted no part of it.

I had very little knowledge of nor experience with the stock market. I knew it could be risky, because my mother had talked about the Depression. Born in 1919, she knew that many had lost their savings in the Stock Market and the bank had foreclosed on the house her father was building for them. The message I got from her was that only gamblers invested in that kind of thing, but I thought it might be an opportunity to turn the money into something more. You just had to be smart about it. I set about educating myself, starting with the business section of the local newspaper. In the 70s, something called an Index Fund was starting to be talked about. The problem with small investors like me was too much risk because of lack of diversity.

Let's say I decide to buy five stocks with the $5000 I got, $1000 in each stock. If one of those stocks went belly up, I would lose 20% of my savings. Now, with the new Index Fund, which spreads the risk over the 500 stocks in the Standard and Poor's—a list of the 500 largest companies listed on the stock market—it is highly unlikely that 20% of those companies would fail. An Index fund seemed to be a fairly safe way of getting involved in the Stock Market.

By 1983, I was working full time as a head proofreader at PicaGraphics, a printer who did ad work and books, mostly college textbooks. Each day I drove past an office that had just opened on Route 59 in Spring Valley. It was a brokerage firm called Gary Goldberg Financial Services.

Around that time, there was an article in the *Journal News* about Goldberg. He was 37, three years younger than I was. He had started out by handing out fliers and talking to shoppers in a supermarket parking lot. I admired such determination and decided that I was ready to take the next step and seek a more sophisticated portfolio.

One afternoon after work I walked into his office, sat down

at his desk, and told him I wanted to open a brokerage account. It was both scary and exciting to step into this unknown territory—to become an actual investor in Mutual Funds, and maybe even individual stocks.

A year later Goldberg purchased a mansion in Rockland County that that he named Montebello. It had belonged to Thomas Fortune Ryan, the Railroad Magnate. My grandmother on my father's side was Elizabeth Ryan. Growing up, I had heard of Thomas Fortune Ryan, had heard that he was a millionaire and was somehow related to my grandmother. The story was that my grandmother had a brother, who was a lawyer and that they had inherited money, but that he had cheated her out of her share. I had done research on the Ryan side of the family over the years and had been unable to find any connection to Thomas Fortune Ryan, but I felt that this coincidence was a good omen.

Only recently did I find a will on a genealogy site of my great-grandmother, Anna Power Ryan. And, indeed, she did own several pieces of property that she left to her son and two daughters, It was quite a lengthy piece of legalese, but it is quite possible that the brother had cheated his sister. So, it appears that part of the story was true.

When my father died in 1970, the Dow Jones was barely near 800. I remember quite clearly the exhilaration I felt that day in January of 1987 when the Dow hit 2000. My father's legacy was on its way.

I have dealt with a number of investment firms and brokers, but I have always had a fondness for Gary Goldberg.

When we lived to Nyack, Ernie and I and a group of friends formed an investment group called Big Bucks and Doughs to educate ourselves and invest in stocks. Later, when we moved to Michigan, I joined an investment group there.

My initial investment was from my father's legacy, but my skill and involvement in investing has developed and our investments have grown because Ernie made a good living at General Motors and we were both savers and added to that legacy over the years.

I've begun to realize that the legacy of my father's hasn't stopped with me, but has continued. Instead of adding to the mess of toys the grandkids received on Christmas and birthdays, Ernie and I decided to open up a trust fund for each of them, which they got when they came of age. Some of them have gotten interested in investing; some got a little better start on life than they would have.

The legacy continues . . .

# Amen

I remember my First Holy Communion, my hands clasped in prayer, my head bowed. The white veil, simple, but trimmed with lace, draped across my shoulders. I remember feeling holy...special...chosen.

We had to confess our sins. Tell the priest all the bad things we had done, so we were pure enough to receive "the body of Christ." My world was simple then. Right and wrong. Good and evil. Black and white.

I think of that day, that feeling, when I go to yoga and stand in prayer pose, hands pressed together over my heart center, feeling strong...wise...powerful. I am older by seventy plus years, therefore I *am* stronger, wiser, more powerful than that six-year-old. But it is more than that. My hands are closer to my chest and are pointed slightly inward, as if the strength is within me, not that I am asking someone else for it. My head instead of being bowed in supplication, subservience, is held high, steady, strong and proud. My feet are planted firmly on the ground.

As a child, I was taught that pride was a sin, one of the seven deadly sins. One of the definitions of pride in the dictionary is "self-esteem, self-respect." I was not a proud girl; I am a proud woman.

I am proud that this aged body can still stand tall and do yoga twice a week. Life's complexities have taught me that things are rarely all right or all wrong; people aren't all good or all evil. I am proud that I have gained this insight through my experiences. I am proud and respect myself; I don't believe this is a sin, but a strength. I don't confess to a priest; I look within and search my soul. My connection is personal, spiritual.

Breathe in. Breathe out. Inhale slowly, deeply.

Head bowed, I pay respect to others—teachers, fellow yogis. It fills my spirit with gratitude, love, and completeness. I feel at one with the universe. My soul honors your soul. And so it is.

Amen.

# NAMASTE

www.ingramcontent.com/pod-product-compliance
Lightning Source LLC
Chambersburg PA
CBHW061249120726
48001CB00001B/222